Space for Grace

Giles Goddard is Chair of Inclusive Church and Rector of St Peter's Church, Walworth in South London. He is an Honorary Canon of Southwark Cathedral.

Related titles available from Canterbury Press

*The Inclusive God: Reclaiming theology for an inclusive
church*
Steven Shakespeare and Hugh Rayment-Pickard
978-1-85311-741-1

Inclusivity has nothing to do with being liberal, it's not a
churchy version of political correctness. It's a gospel imperative, fundamental to the nature of God and at the very heart
of the mission and ministry of our Lord Jesus Christ.
Giles Fraser, writer and broadcaster

Prayers for an Inclusive Church
Steven Shakespeare
978-1-85311-915-6

Space for Grace

Creating inclusive churches

Giles Goddard

CANTERBURY
PRESS
Norwich

© Giles Goddard 2008

First published in 2008 by the Canterbury Press Norwich
(a publishing imprint of Hymns Ancient & Modern Limited,
a registered charity)
13–17 Long Lane, London ECIA 9PN

www.scm-canterburypress.co.uk

Scripture quotations are from the New Revised Standard Version
of the Bible, copyright 1989 by the Division of Christian Education
of the National Council of the Churches of Christ in the USA.
Used by permission. All rights reserved.

British Library Cataloguing in Publication data

A catalogue record for this book is available
from the British Library

ISBN 978-1-85311-916-3

Typeset by Regent Typesetting, London
Printed in the UK by CPI William Clowes
Beccles NR34 7TL

Enlarge the site of your tent,
and let the curtains of your habitations be stretched out;
do not hold back, lengthen your cords
and strengthen your stakes.

Isaiah 54.2

Whenever we are presented with a choice
between being biblical and being inclusive,
it is a false dichotomy –
for to be truly biblical is to be inclusive
in any community which wants to follow and imitate
Jesus.

Richard Burridge, *Imitating Jesus*

Contents

Foreword

Giles Goddard and I began talking about 'inclusiveness' when the Church Commissioners sold the Octavia Hill Estates in London in a way that could exclude future generations of the community he serves from ever becoming tenants there. Out of this came many discussions and debates with him and with the movement called Inclusive Church, which owes much to his inspiration; for inclusiveness is no simple matter.

There are many routes by which people learn the difference between including and excluding, between being included and being excluded. Some are pleasant and some unpleasant, some intellectual and some emotional, some constructive and some destructive. This book charts many of these routes for the journey of discovery, and may include those you have travelled, or are travelling.

Some routes involve the difficult decisions that have to be taken by people in authority; in which including everyone is seldom an option. You will read here how a parish priest and his churchwardens and Church Council struggle with the dilemmas such decisions can have on a community or on an individual.

Not all people are in a position to make such decisions; usually our experience is as the recipient of others' decisions to include or exclude us. This book is written with a gay person's awareness of the types of exclusion to be encountered in our culture and in most churches. The stories that begin the chapters of this book are told with the empathy that comes from such personal experience.

These stories, mostly from life at St Peter's Walworth in London, are not told for their own sake, but as representations of the wider struggles about inclusion and exclusion within society generally, and specifically within the life of the Anglican Communion of which St Peter's is part, and which the author loves and serves. In the telling of these stories Giles Goddard invites us to see in microcosm the wider political and ecclesial struggles in which he is involved: struggles about inclusion, its dilemmas and opportunities, its turbulence and delights.

Such an account, written by a Christian priest, cannot draw only on his own and his contemporaries' experiences in reaching its conclusions. This is at its heart a theological book: one that engages not just with contemporary experience but with the record of Christian faith, and especially with the biblical testimony. Predominantly it engages with Jesus Christ, the one who in being excluded opened wide his arms on the Cross to embrace all his brothers and sisters. It is the conviction of the author that the passion to include is deep in the heart of God, and therefore belongs in every human heart too.

This conviction, born of personal engagement with the life and teaching of Christ, as person, Christian and priest, does not in any way deny the ambiguities and dilemmas that are intrinsic to the passion to include. Instead it tackles some of the difficult questions. Are there no limits to inclusion? Is not exclusion sometimes required? Is there not as much exclusion as inclusion in the testimony of the Old and the New Testaments? So the reader must expect that the 'hard texts' are there to be wrestled with, as well as the well-known texts to which those seeking to commend a gospel of inclusion will readily refer.

The reader will be in no doubt about the main tensions that underlie this book: Giles Goddard is committed to an Anglican faith that is generous and resists the instinct to exclude on the basis of disagreement or difference, that doesn't draw boundaries around the Communion in the quest for a 'pure' Church that permits only one interpretation of Christ's teaching. What this book makes clear is that this is no mere political stance in a current (let us hope, transient) church struggle. In his hopes for the Anglican Communion, the author sees the outworking of his commitment to Christian faith, and the echo of constant themes in the life of his parish.

This book challenges its readers to discern in personal experience and in the life of their communities the outworking of God's passionate love for all humankind, a love that contrives to be ultimately demanding and all-embracing at the same time. They will be glad to know that in the difficulties in the way of that vision they have the companionship of many who, like Giles Goddard, have committed themselves to a ministry that reaches out in the name of the one whose ambition for humankind is that none should be lost.

Peter Selby

Peter Selby is Visiting Professor in the Department of Theology and Religious Studies and the International Centre for Prison Studies at King's College, London, and a former Bishop of Worcester.

Acknowledgements

Much of what happens in this book was worked out in tandem with the growth and development of Inclusive Church, and I'm grateful to all those who have at any time served on the Executive Committee or played a part in its life – especially Giles Fraser, Erica Wooff, Philip Chester, Alex Campbell and Christina Rees.

Thanks to Peter Selby for his constant wisdom, example and advice. Sharon Moughtin-Mumby ploughed through the first draft and made many helpful comments, and has brought great inspiration to St Peter's during her time so far as curate.

To write a book while trying to take care of a parish requires patience and understanding – on the part of the parish. I'm grateful to all the congregation of St Peter's, especially Catherine Attride our wonderful administrator, Alan Wild and Sheila Saunders the honorary curates, and Toro Erogbogbo and Margaret Goodson who were churchwardens for most of the time this book was developing. Their support and commitment has been tremendous.

Above all thanks to everyone who's gone before, and everyone around the world, struggling in ways much harder than I can imagine to make sure that the Christian churches play their part in celebrating the gospel of welcome.

Introduction

It was only as I was writing this book that I began to understand how fundamental and how transformative inclusive theology can be. Practice and comprehension are two very different things. An instinct to include does not necessarily understand the imperative or the theology that underpin it. So I plead guilty to having acted from instinct – from an awareness that Jesus came to call not the saved but the lost – without serious reflection on the implications of his call.

But I was also aware of a gap in the market. Most of the literature available on these subjects (and there is a swiftly increasing amount of a very high standard) is written by professional theologians and scholars, offering coherent resources to those of us working in parishes and church communities across the country, but without necessarily drawing the direct connections between the gospel message and the places where we live and work.

Hence this book. The complexities of Christian ministry are great. All those with responsibility for ministry, whether lay or ordained, liturgical or pastoral, are aware of the intersecting tangle of dynamics that surround even the simplest act. Who has not been caught up in the politics of the flower rota, or dismayed by an unexpected rejection of what seems like an obvious change? Simply to say 'We want to be an inclusive church' is rarely enough.

In this book I attempt to make the connections between the life and work of a particular church community in a particular place and the implications of the inclusive imperative. In drawing out the threads of inclusion, I hope to try to untangle the web of dynamics in a way that responds to the call of Jesus in the streets and communities in which we work.

My parish, St Peter's Walworth, is near the Elephant and Castle in South London. It is an ordinary parish in an ordinary part of London; poorer and more ethnically mixed than average, but with most of the challenges and potential that any church community has. I focus on it not because I think it has any particular significance, but because it is the one parish I know well, and it is the place where I have tried to put into action my understanding of the faith to which we are called. My years of ministry at St Peter's have been a time of discovery. The desire I share with most of the congregation – to be a church that is open, caring and prayerful – has led us into unknown places where we have all learnt from each other. Change and resist-ance, fears and hope have worked together in a process that has at times been difficult and at times very exciting. I don't think that the experience of St Peter's is unique – my hope is that the universal aspects of what we've tried to learn will resonate with others, whether they're in Puddletown or Princeton or Perth; because although the locations and personalities are different, the issues are often the same.

St Peter's is an Anglican parish, and this book is written in an Anglican context. I take seriously the notion of the Anglican theological method – the 'milking stool' of scripture, reason and tradition, whose interplay enables us continually to reflect on what we learn from scripture in the light of tradition using our reason. I deliberately do not include experience as a fourth leg, not just because it spoils the milking stool analogy but because I believe that it is an essential part of all three elements. The notion that we can come at scripture unaffected by our cul-tural, social, political and personal context is not sustainable. We understand tradition in the light of our experience; the way in which we view the history of the place of women in society, for instance, is inextricable from the place we believe women should now occupy. Reason and experience, too, are bound up together; cultural context and intellectual reflection are locked in a sometimes virtuous and sometimes vicious circle. The ex-

clusion of black people was thought, by impeccably reasonable
people, to be intellectually justifiable for 300 years (from the
sixteenth to the mid-twentieth century), but as the experience
and voices of black people have begun to be heard in a less
imperialist world, similarly impeccably reasonable people have
realized how unsustainable exclusion is.

This realization has crucial implications for our understanding of scripture. This book seeks to base all of its conclusions on
a rigorous understanding of what we learn from the Bible as the
key text in the interpretation of the central event in Christianity
– the life, death and resurrection of Jesus the Christ. But one
of the main reasons for the mess in which the churches are at
the moment is the idea, which has emerged in recent centuries
among particular groups of Christians, that there is only one
possible interpretation of scripture, which is self-evidently true.
That if only we can get back to 'What scripture really says', we
will be true believers; and anyone who disagrees with us will be
a false prophet. *Anathemus sit*. Let her be outcast.

The implications of this sort of 'textual foundationalism'[1] or
'historical criticism'[2] are well described by Dale Martin in his
recent book, *Sex and the Single Savior*, to which I refer later.
The consequences are around us; the solution is within us. As
Rowan Williams says, 'When Christian speech is healthy, it does
not allow itself an over-familiarity with, a taking for granted
of its images, its scriptures, its art, its liturgy – it is prepared
to draw back to allow them to be "strange", questioning and

---

1 Textual foundationalism acknowledges the reader's culture and
situation in the interpretation of texts, but holds that there is one original meaning which it is possible to uncover. Dale Martin speaks of the
'myth of textual agency' – the common assumption that 'the Bible
"speaks" and our job is just to listen'. Dale Martin, *Sex and the Single
Savior*, 1.

2 Historical criticism is literary criticism based on the historical context of a work and its author, as opposed to criticism based upon the
language or form of the text. Historical criticism holds that it is possible
to identify the meaning and intention of a text in a way unaffected by
the reader's culture and situation.

questionable.'[3] The Bible is a collection of writings by human beings inspired by God, who are seeking to make sense of the inexplicable, and to encapsulate the infinite. The salvation event of God's in-breaking into the world, with all that it implies, cannot be summed up in a series of factual statements like a technical manual.

Therefore I take the Bible seriously but not simply. Each chapter of this book begins with the experience or story of a member of St Peter's congregation. It reflects on a particular aspect of ministry in the light of the Bible and of the tradition; and it seeks to draw out the implications of inclusion as it has been worked out in the parish. Not as an instruction book, but as a way of demonstrating how we in our part of London have tried to respond to our understanding of the gospel.

Chapter 1, 'What is it with you lot?', looks at the way in which individual human rights have come to the fore since the Second World War, and considers the interplay between these and the church as the body of Christ, and the church as community. Chapter 2, 'A Quiet Transformation?', looks at the opportunities and difficulties around making changes in church. Chapter 3, 'The Inclusive Imperative', develops the argument that inclusion is at the heart of the gospel of love. Chapter 4, 'Remove Packaging Before Use', reflects on how contemporary society, with its fragmentation of traditional identities and rise of new ways of talking about 'truth', impacts on the churches. Chapter 5, 'Shall I be leader?', asks how Christian leadership is affected by the inclusive imperative, and Chapter 6, 'Limitless Freedom?', considers where the limits of inclusion lie (if such limits exist). The interlocking structures of oppression are considered in Chapters 7, 'From the Margins to the Centre', and 8, 'Them out there, us in here'. They look at the three areas where the struggle has been greatest – black and minority ethnic people, women, and gay, lesbian, bisexual and transgendered ('queer') Christians. Chapter 9, 'My Space, Your Space', was originally published in Malcolm Terry's *Regeneration and Renewal*. It

---

3 Larkin-Stuart Lecture, Toronto, 16 April 2007.

tells the story of how we tried to make the building of St Peter's more inclusive and more responsive for the local community. The Conclusion recalls the vision with which we are entrusted.

Although not explicitly about evangelism, the whole book is shot through with a consciousness of our task – to communicate the gospel of love to those we serve. The call to full inclusion is part and parcel of the mission of the church; the public perception of the church as a place not of welcome but of rejection is partly to blame for the decline in numbers. If we are to reverse the decline, a first step must be the removal of obstacles that stand in the way of the work of the Spirit in the church and the world. Inclusion and evangelism are intricately linked.

Space restrictions have not allowed reflection on people of other faiths, or any serious drawing out of the implications of inclusion for global justice, for creation and the environment, and for other traditionally excluded groups – including children and young people, the elderly and those with disabilities. But I've probably tried to do much in too small a space already, and hope that it will be clear from what follows how these questions might be tackled in an inclusive church community.

This book was written at the beginning of my tenth year as Rector of St Peter's. There has, genuinely, never been a dull moment. The gifts, talents and generosity of the members of the congregation – those who were alongside me since the beginning and those who joined since – have been nothing short of astonishing, and I'm deeply grateful for all that we have worked through, together. I'm quite sure I have misrepresented them and some of our experiences, and apologize for that. But it is with a strong sense that, under the guidance of the Holy Spirit, we have moved forward into places where we never thought we'd go; and so it is, of course, to the people of St Peter's that this book is dedicated.

Giles Goddard
London
Ascensiontide 2008

I

'What is it with you lot?'

But God has so arranged the body, giving the greater honour to the inferior member, that there may be no dissension within the body, but the members may have the same care for one another. If one member suffers, all suffer together with it; if one member is honoured, all rejoice together with it.
1 Corinthians 12.24–26

We are the body of Christ. In the one Spirit we were all baptized into the one body. Let us then pursue all that makes for peace and builds up our common life.[1]

Of the many ills perceived to be affecting our society at the moment, one of the greatest is fragmentation. Harsh comparisons are drawn with some previous period or different country, in whose villages everyone takes care of everyone else and doors can be left unlocked all day without fear of burglary; where the street is a safe place and families eat, breathe and live closely together in a solid and stable community of support and care.

The seminal sociological study by Michael Young and Peter Willmott, *Family and Kinship in East London*, paints a picture of such a time, when the mother–daughter relationship was the defining structure in most families, and when it was not unusual for family members not living in the same household to see each other two, three or four times a day. And we are often told of the way in which children are reared in villages in Africa, where discipline and support are shared among the community and each child is the responsibility of all.

To be sure, these pictures of life in a bygone age or a distant place are viewed through spectacles heavily tinted. There was,

---

1 *Common Worship*, Eucharist Order 1, Contemporary language.

briefly, a low crime rate in London in the 1950s; but the nine-teenth and early twentieth centuries were no time to be out on the streets late at night. The 1950s were a time of shock and recovery after the cataclysm that was the Second World War. Village life may indeed in many ways offer security and com-munity, but woe betide those who fall out of favour with that community, or who do not fit in, or who are rejected because of their difference. The village structure on the islands of West-ern Samoa is remarkable in its strength and stability; but those who do not wish or who are unable to conform, for whatever reason, are soon exiled to the island's capital, Apia, where their residence is often hand-to-mouth since a community of support hardly exists there.

Comparisons between the twenty-first century and the 1950s, or with small subsistence communities from any age, are like comparing mangoes and hazelnuts. The changes that have taken place across the world over the last 50 years have been exponen-tially greater in almost every way than the changes that affected societies in the centuries before. Travel, technology, migration, the position of women, the recognition of human rights, the acknowledgement of same-sex gender attraction and love, the recognition of the equality of different ethnic groups, universal suffrage as a pre-condition for democracy – all of these have in different ways contributed to the transformation of society in ways undreamt of by philosophers, theologians, sociologists or policy-makers as little as 50 years ago.

We are, indeed, in a brave new world. We are in a world char-acterized by diversity and difference, by instability and innova-tion. We are in a world that, by and large, celebrates the onward march of capitalism and the gifts it offers – the availability of mass tourism, the instant access to information and entertain-ment, the fluidity and flux of fashion, the availability of luxury and comfort on a level inconceivable even to our grandparents.

Above all, the greatest change, certainly in western societies, has been the recognition that the individual has rights over and against the community, and that no one should be disadvantaged by society because of any factor inherent in their birth; whether that is to do with their gender, ethnicity, sexual orientation, whether they are rich or poor, able or have a disability. Articles 1 and 2 of the United Nations Declaration of Human Rights read:

Article 1

All human beings are born free and equal in dignity and rights. They are endowed with reason and conscience and should act towards one another in a spirit of brotherhood.

Article 2

Everyone is entitled to all the rights and freedoms set forth in this Declaration, without distinction of any kind, such as race, colour, sex, language, religion, political or other opinion, national or social origin, property, birth or other status. Furthermore, no distinction shall be made on the basis of the political, jurisdictional or international status of the country or territory to which a person belongs, whether it be independent, trust, non-self-governing or under any other limitation of sovereignty.

In the middle of all this – or, rather, increasingly on the edge of all this – lies the church. Established millennia ago, on a model that owes more to empire and to Roman jurisdiction than to anything that has transformed society in the last ten decades, being primarily a patriarchal institution with a clear hierarchy of bishops, priests and laity (or in the Reformed tradition, ministers and laity), the church is finding itself increasingly exposed to the chill winds of modernity without the resources to be able to respond.

Its language, culture, self-understanding and history are all derived from a way of being that is increasingly out of step with the world it tries to serve. Like a cathedral on a hill, it is buffeted and battered by wind and rain, and sometimes it seems as if the only response it can make is to close its doors and try to turn the heating up, in the hope that those inside won't hear the storm or feel the cold.

It reads its source documents – the scriptures – through the eyes of its history, and sees in them justifications for its past behaviour rather than enlightenment on how it might respond to the present. In so doing it undermines its past and denies its present, with the result that the future is at best a shadowy possibility and at worst non-existent.

Of course, this is a caricature. There have been major and significant changes in the life of the church; the recognition of lay responsibility in the structures of the church, the ordination of women to the priesthood in England and to the episcopate in other Anglican provinces and other denominations; the end of apartheid in South Africa and the recognition of the equality of people from different ethnicities across the western churches; the updating of liturgy and worship so that it is in the language and media of the present rather than the past, and, above all, the constant background noise of discussion, debate and controversy as to how far future changes might take the church.

But these changes have, by and large, been slow, late and grudging. They have come about as a result of enormous pressure for change, and the leaders of the church have rarely been at the forefront of that pressure. Self-preservation more than prophecy has in many cases been a motivating factor, and instead of offering a new vision for a new society, all too often the old vision has been re-offered in a slightly different pattern or colourway.

The sadness is that the new vision is right at the heart of the church's faith. One of the most striking innovations in the Church of England's liturgy was brought in during the 1960s, to strong resistance at the time, but now welcomed as an intrinsic part of the liturgy – the peace. In exchanging the peace with one another, we are explicitly acknowledging the essential truth of the words: 'We *are* the body of Christ. In one Spirit we were all baptized into one body. Let us then pursue *all* that makes for peace and builds up our common life.'[2]

The scriptures should be documents of liberation, not oppression. Within them, in the words used at services of ordination, is contained 'all that is necessary for salvation', if they can be read and understood fully and completely. They are the written expression of hundreds of years' attempts to understand God, and God's relationship with humanity and the world. As such,

---

2 *Common Worship*, Eucharist Order 1, Contemporary language. Italics mine.

their contents are astonishingly diverse – ranging from history to poetry, and from story to law.

We, as readers of the Bible, do not come to it like blank canvases. We bring our cultural background, language, expectations and preconceptions. We understand the past through the lens of the present, and we interpret scripture through the lens of our faith and of our world. What is happening when we read the Bible is that we are entering into a relationship with the text that is before us, and with the almost always anonymous authors of the text; the past meets the future in the present, and we as readers are shaped by and shape our understandings of the words we read.

Scripture is not, in other words, a telephone directory; neither is it the Highway Code. Much reading of the Bible in recent years, particularly in the last century, was with the aim of finding the 'original meaning' of the passage, through various types of critical method – especially 'historical criticism'.[3] But it is not possible to find our way back to the 'original meaning' any more than it is possible to understand how, say, the first hearers of Beethoven's Fifth Symphony would have heard the music. We cannot take ourselves out of our context; but this is a virtue, not a vice. For the Bible speaks now as then in all its richness and depth. One of the sad things about the present situation facing the church is that many of those who have strong views, especially of a conservative hue, have in some ways reduced the scriptures to a version of an ethical code that conforms to their understanding of ethics, and this tragically distorts and diminishes the richness and depths of God's Word.

The Christian tradition contains a constant undertone of

---

3 'In sum, when apologists for historical criticism say that history is necessary because Christianity is an historical religion, they are using the term "history" in two very different ways: one to refer to something as having happened in the past, and the other to a set of disciplinary practices and rules. History, in the latter sense, as a *discipline, cannot* serve as the epistemological foundation for theology, nor should Christians insist that the "historical-critical" meaning of the biblical text serve as a *necessary foundation* for theological use of scripture' (Dale Martin, *Sex and the Single Savior*, 14).

challenge and liberty, of saints and activists who went out into the world and tried to live out the vision of the new Jerusalem; the gruff and the joyful, Octavia Hill and St Francis, F. D. Maurice and Mother Julian of Norwich. The onward march of reason and rationality, through the Reformation into the Enlightenment and on into modernity and postmodernity, has carried theologians and thinkers with it. We have increasingly begun to interpret and to understand God not as the patriarch portrayed by Michelangelo but as the undefinable defined of the early Fathers. There is a school of early theology (the 'apophatic' school) that holds that it is only possible to say what God is not, rather than what God is. The paternalistic but judgemental image of God associated with the Middle Ages has developed into a conception of God that is harder to picture and less like an angry headmaster – and faith and theology continue to develop.

* * *

The metaphor of the body is perhaps the most commonly used biblical metaphor for the Church. There are many others – the vine, the flock, the City of God, the *ekklesia* or assembly; but the body has such deep resonances that it has continued as a defining symbol and identification of the nature of church. It is a metaphor, an analogy, often used within the New Testament; it is certainly the metaphor with which Paul is most comfortable and that he uses most often in his passionate, argumentative, determined and inspiring letters to the communities of followers of Christ which he established.

Paul's use of the image of the body contains within it, in embryo, all the theological insights which are creeping up almost unnoticed on the church today. The insights which will, once we begin to take them seriously, offer a way of being church in the world which is both coherent and rational, which responds to the insights of the twentieth century without throwing out the depth of theological understanding which enlightened the nineteen centuries before. It is within the metaphor of the body that, implicitly, the fundamentals of the UN Declaration of Human

Rights can be found, establishing the equality and dignity of humanity on the basic Christian understanding that humans are created in the *imago dei* – image of God – and that as such they form part of the body of Christ.

> Indeed, the body does not consist of one member, but of many. If the foot were to say, 'Because I am not a hand, I do not belong to the body', that would not make it any less a part of the body. And if the ear were to say, 'Because I am not an eye, I do not belong to the body', that would not make it any less a part of the body. If the whole body were an eye, where would the hearing be? If the whole body were hearing, where would the sense of smell be?'
>
> 1 Corinthians 12.14–17

The idea of inclusion, when applied to Christianity, has on many occasions been dismissed as an uncritical importation of the human rights agenda into the church. Its critics have sought to reduce its significance by identifying inclusion with a liberal, secular agenda without scriptural foundation, going on to say that it is neither biblical nor justified by the tradition of the church. Those of us who call for a fully inclusive church are called 'revisionists', as opposed to the 'reasserters' who feel called to reassert the fundamentals of the Christian faith.

The metaphor of the body, containing as it does the idea of creation being by its very nature diverse and interdependent, is at once the most traditional, most radical and most generous understanding of church imaginable. Traditional, because it recognizes the eucharistic centre of the church in the life, death and resurrection of Christ who instituted the Eucharist. Radical, because the body in order to survive and thrive is continually regenerating itself, continually changing, continually growing – and yet remaining the same. Generous, because it contains within it the recognition of our deep and undeniable mutual interdependence, as Paul recognizes:

> But God has so arranged the body, giving the greater honour to the inferior member, that there may be no dissension within the body, but the members may have the same care for

one another. If one member suffers, all suffer together with it; if one member is honoured, all rejoice together with it.

1 Corinthians 12.24–26

Inclusion is at the heart of Paul's theology. He it is who says to the Corinthians:

God chose what is foolish in the world to shame the wise; God chose what is weak in the world to shame the strong; God chose what is low and despised in the world, things that are not, to reduce to nothing things that are, so that no one might boast in the presence of God.

1 Corinthians 1.27–29

He recognizes that the gospel brings in the outcast and the rejected – 'Not many of you were wise by human standards, not many were powerful, not many were of noble birth' (1 Corinthians 1.26) – so that the new world order can be created and the gospel can be seen to be at work, here, on earth, among the people of God and in the body of Christ.

Of course, there are parts of Paul's letters which appear to be the opposite of inclusive; the apparent condemnation of same-sex relationships in Romans 1.27, the very clear instructions on the behaviour of women at, for example, 1 Corinthians 11.2–6 and 1 Corinthians 14.33–36. Any attempt to argue for a vision of a church which is truly welcoming of all must take these sections of scripture seriously.

But equally, both the Gospels and the Epistles are very clear in their call for the inclusion of all people, whether they are rich (Zacchaeus) or poor (the Syro-Phoenician woman) – whether they are part of the establishment (Nicodemus) or part of the underclass (the woman at the well) – whether they are Jew or Gentile, slave or free, male or female. A foundational message of the New Testament is that all are one in Christ Jesus.

* * *

Yugoslavia, before the death of General Tito. Many different groups – Serbian, Croatian, Muslim – live alongside one another, apparently in harmony and apparently working well together. Dissent is suppressed and genuine encounter not encouraged, in a police state where the power rests entirely with the dictator, the Communist Party and the secret service. Almost immediately after Tito's death, the country erupts into violence; quickly, new states are formed – Slovenia, Croatia – and then follows the absolute horror of the Balkans, the terrible ethnic cleansing, the massacres and violence and rape and slaughter.

In the middle of all this, Miroslav Volf, a Croatian theologian now working in the United States, asks: 'How can I love my enemy?' How, he asks, can I love the person who is living on the land which was mine, who has stolen my livelihood and might have killed my brother or raped my mother?

His book *Exclusion and Embrace* is an extended theological reflection on the 'history of vicious cultural, ethnic, and racial strife'[4] that has characterized the three areas with which Volf was particularly concerned at the time of writing the book: Sarajevo, Los Angeles and Berlin. The particular challenge he poses is to try to make sense of the great commandment to 'love your enemy' in the context of the Yugoslavian descent into violence and murder, but there can hardly be said to be a place in the world which does not at some level have a history of violence, oppression and exclusion.

It may be thought extreme to compare an English parish to Sarajevo, but the conclusions Volf reaches have resonances for the most mild-mannered congregation in the outer reaches of the English countryside. Of particular relevance is his meditation on the nature of 'embrace', to which he comes after detailed consideration of the causes and consequences of the exclusion of the other to which human society seems to be endemically committed.

> But while he was still far off, his father saw him and was filled with compassion; he ran and put his arms around him and kissed him.
> Luke 15.20

---

4 Miroslav Volf, *Exclusion and Embrace*, 14.

The human tendency to create groups and communities of identity, whether it be membership of the golf club or the dramatic society, membership of one street gang over against another, or membership of one ethnic group fighting with another for the same land, is an outworking of our ability to conceive of ourselves as individuals alongside other individuals, with some of whom we identify and some of whom we reject. Our separation from one another is, in the Christian narrative, a reflection of our separation from God; and it is only through union with God that we can achieve union with one another. The liberation theologian Gustavo Gutiérrez writes, 'The deepest root of all servitude is the breaking of friendship with God and with other human beings, and cannot therefore be eradicated except by the unmerited redemptive love of the Lord whom we receive by faith and in communion with one another.'[5]

'When we were still far off, you met us in your Son and brought us home.'[6] The action of embrace, according to Volf, has four component parts: first, opening the arms. Second, waiting. Third, closing the arms. And fourth, opening them again. In these four actions we both engage with and acknowledge the identity of the other. By opening the arms, we invite the other to come towards us. By waiting, we allow them to make their decision, freely, whether to receive the love we offer and to offer love themselves. By closing the arms, we acknowledge the giving and the receiving of love. And by opening them again, we allow the other to continue to be the individual we have embraced, but in a new relationship which acknowledges our interdependence and our mutual love.

It is in the embrace between the alienated father and son, or in the embrace of Jesus on the cross ('He opened wide his arms for us upon the cross'[7]) that we find the core of the life of the Christian community, the parish, the church congregation. We are, in the end, a sacramental community which derives its

---

5 Gustavo Gutiérrez, *Theology of Liberation*, xxxviii.

6 *Common Worship*, Eucharistic Prayer Order 1, Contemporary language.

7 Eucharistic Prayer B.

being, its sense of existential status, from the two sacraments of baptism and communion; and of these two, communion most profoundly symbolizes and expresses the radical renewal of the relationship of love to which we are called.

* * *

An Anglican parish church, in a city suburb. Sunday morning, before the main service at 10.30. Somebody is preparing the service sheets. Somebody else is setting up the altar. A couple of people are organizing Junior Church, and two other people are deep in discussion about the coffee rota. The clergy are wandering around getting under people's feet, and the organist arrives, late, and breathlessly looks for the hymn tunes in the old book because the new one has gone missing. Someone wanders in off the street wanting to know if we're Anglican or Catholic, and a long-standing family (grandmother, 93, mother, 61, daughter, 33, granddaughter, 11) make their stately way up the church steps bidding a gracious good morning to all they meet.

In that small cast of characters we have: four Sierra Leoneans; one Nigerian woman (bisexual); two gay men; two white working-class women (one clergy, one lay); one white working-class man (clergy, straight); one woman with long-term mental health problems; one man (divorced) recently married to his divorced partner and looking after his mother who has Alzheimer's; one young middle-class woman who is avowedly atheist but celebrates the church community; and two Nigerian matriarchs who see themselves as responsible for the smooth running of the church, come what may.

As the congregation starts to arrive, so the diversity grows. Age, wealth, social status, employment, sexual orientation, ability; all are thrown into the melting pot, and in the chatter and the praying, the singing and the hearing, the ingredients begin to meld. The disparate become one, and the individuals become a community. Briefly, in the moment after the Eucharist, there is a silence. And, perhaps, in that silence, broken maybe by a baby crying or by the sneeze of an old lady with a cold, the community acknowledges itself as a communion, and has a sense of itself as something beyond itself, as a reflection (however muddied, however pale) of the kingdom of God we are called to celebrate.

By the end of the notices the sense of unity is going; by coffee time it's almost gone. But there's a memory, still, of the sense of the glory of the presence of the Lord that will linger and grow week by week. So, gradually, the community builds; we *are* the body of Christ, and we *are becoming* the body of Christ.

A happy accident? A simple reflection of a local event, with no significance beyond the way in which this church attempts to serve the people of its parish? Something unachievable in more monochrome, more unified areas where the population is universally reasonably well off and predominantly white? Or something more significant?

It is in the richness and diversity of church congregations that the body of Christ is reflected. At the heart of the gospel is the incarnation, with all that it tells us about the love of God for the world God created, and the crucifixion, death and resurrection of Christ. The world God created in its infinite beauty and indescribable diversity, where each of us, from the ant to the elephant and from the amoeba to Alpha Centauri, is inextricably co-dependent, individual, different and united. The church, at its best, is called to celebrate that; because the church is both a gift of God in creation and a vision of the new Jerusalem.

The imperative implicit within the metaphor of the body is that the people who make up the church recognize the depth of their interdependence. We are not like a skip left outside a house under renovation, being filled indiscriminately with bits of old tile, a broken sofa, a couple of tin teapots and a great deal of rubble. Although the diversity of a church community is usually a reflection of the area in which that community is placed, the challenge laid upon us is to turn the happy accident into a positive virtue; to create something out of nothing, to transform a mixed group of individuals into something with a significance beyond itself, which, in its relationships and its commitment, models and reflects the relationship and the commitment of Jesus to the world he loves.

You may be thinking: 'Our church is not like that. Our area is not mixed; our people are all from similar social backgrounds, share a commonality of interests, are fairly monochrome – what is the inclusive imperative for us?' But all is never as it seems. The assumption of similarity can obscure the recognition that even if diversity is not so immediately visible, within every con-gregation is a mix and a melting pot of home situations, of per-sonality types, of characters, of political and social views which, if unrecognized, can mean that the *ekklesia*, the assembly, will be unable to move beyond a largely superficial way of relating. Then, differences of opinion may be shoved firmly under the carpet, resulting in a non-engagement that, in its way, can be deeply counterproductive – even destructive, if conformity is bought at the cost of honesty. Or there is the contrary danger, in a place where diversity is obvious and all the 'inclusion' boxes can be ticked, that although lip service is paid to the need to communicate and engage, there is little beyond superficial ac-knowledgement of the multifarious people around. The result, similarly, is stasis.

The life of the parish is both banal and cosmic; both mundane and transcendent. Behind the arguments about the coffee rota, the annual donations to international development projects, the common round of hymns and visits and parties and parish projects and visits by the bishop, lies the consciousness of the possibility of a radical, renewed and reinvigorated relationship between God and humanity, a transformation of all that drives us apart –

'We *are* the body of Christ. In the one Spirit we were *all* bap-tized into the one body. Let us then pursue all that makes for peace and builds up our common life.'[8]

---

8 *Common Worship*, Eucharist Order 1, Contemporary language (my italics).

2

A Quiet Transformation?

Sheila Saunders was born in 1942 in South London. Part of a large family, she won a prize, aged nine, for taking the most children to Sunday school. One day she was playing with a Roman Catholic child who was sent to church. Sheila went with her. A nun told her to wait outside. 'I remember what I thought. I asked God to confirm to me that this building I had been told not to enter, belonged to him and was for everyone. Knowing the answer was yes, I had to go in to prove a point to myself and to this nun.'

Twenty-five years later she moved to the other end of the parish. Her own children started going to the youth club at St Peter's. 'I remember them coming home and saying they'd been taught to gamble. They were playing roulette. I was shocked. But I thought I'd better start going to church there. I remember the first time I went. There were people at the door giving out sheets. They'd see you, a stranger, and their face dropped. I'd never come across so much hostility towards a stranger. Because it was hostile I thought, "I'm staying." There was one black lady there. We made sandwiches for the fête. No one else would work with her. I took tea round to the stall holders and it was like, "Who the hell are you?" One woman just ignored me. "Perhaps she's deaf." She turned out later to be lovely, but it took a long time. There was another fête. There were two black ladies, and they were given the jumble. They were stuck outside by the boiler room. I went to work with them and we took some of the jumble into the main hall. "This needs changing" I said to myself. "I can't stand by and watch it." The PCC (church council) was made up of the in-crowd and if you weren't in it you weren't in.

'I was made churchwarden. I think Paul [Jobson – rector 1971–90] realized things needed to change and expected me to do it for him. Jack [Smoker, the other churchwarden] wouldn't talk to me for a year.'

Sheila and Jack were joint churchwardens for 16 years. About two years after I took up the post of Rector, Jack became 'Clerk of Works' responsible for the day-to-day maintenance of the church. Two new churchwardens were elected, and Sheila started training for ordination.

'I never believed that people could really be like that. I think it's fear – the way people react to people in power. When the priest before you came he treated everyone the same. Alleluia! Some people left. But for the ones who stayed things changed at once. More black people came. More people did things in services. Gordon and Barbara made the church turn the corner.

'The church does more with the past than it should. The past seems to take precedence. When I was young the church was *the past*. As a child we weren't invited into the congregation. The children were at the back. Even if the lights were on it was as if they'd been turned off as you walked in. When the place opened up, a few years ago, it was like clean water going into a pond. Filling it up with clean water so all the stagnant bits got washed away. The tradition hasn't changed but the cobwebs have been dusted off.'

* * *

It is part of the human condition both to fear the future and to welcome it. To draw back from the challenges and uncertainties which may lie, hidden, just around the corner; but also to tread with hope the path which takes us on. 'Not for ever by still waters would we idly rest and stay' goes the hymn – 'but the steep and rugged pathway may we tread rejoicingly.'

The relationship between fear of the future and welcome for the new things which are to emerge has been played out, again and again, since the beginning of organized religion. It is one of the paradoxes that reside at the heart of Christianity. How shall the first be last and the last first? How can Christ's yoke be easy and his burden light? How shall we deny ourselves? How can Jesus Christ be both fully human and fully divine?

We have been content to recognize that some of the questions with which Christianity confronts us must remain unexplained. The words of the Nicene Creed remain fundamental to any expression of the Christian faith because they describe Christ's nature in a way which does not limit it. 'God from God, light from light, very God from very God, begotten not made, being of one substance with the Father, by whom all things were made.' Attempts to define what is meant by these words quickly run into the sand, and although many have tried, no explanation or development has gone beyond the essential mystery expressed in the Creeds.

As well as doctrinal mysteries, there are dynamic tensions that are built into the core of our common life – for example, between power and powerlessness. Within an institution a hierarchy is almost inevitable, with the consequential differences in the possession and wielding of power. But we are called as Christians to relinquish power, to turn the other cheek, to be last as the first shall be last. How are these to be reconciled?

One of the greatest – perhaps the very greatest – sources of disharmony within Christianity is the tension between tradition and innovation, between the old and the new. Built into the DNA of Christianity is the belief that there is something which is changeless and immutable. The ancient Greek philosophers recognized a fundamental truth when they suggested that the world is in a constant state of flux – the cosmos is made up of fire, said Heraclitus, always changing. But with Plato came a radical revision of that belief; he replaced flux with form, the indefinite with the static. Behind all that we see and experience, thought Plato, lie the 'forms' – the 'real' – and it is the task of philosophy, of knowledge, of religion, to move from the unreal and changing world to the constancy and deep reality which lies behind it. Christianity, heavily influenced by Greek philosophy, seeks the impassable, the eternal. God the Father, the abiding, the uncreated creator – the anchor, truth.

At the same time Christianity is a historical religion. It holds that God acts in the world. It comes directly out of the history of the Hebrews. The story of the people who God called out of Egypt and led into the wilderness, who gained the Promised Land and then were exiled from it; who built the temple in Jerusalem and then stood by, helpless, as the temple was destroyed and they were scattered to the four winds. What defines Christianity is not a book, dictated by God's angel to his last prophet. It is not a relationship with a piece of land, promised by God to his people. It is a historic event – the life, death and resurrection of Jesus Christ, which took place at a certain time in a certain place and changed the course of humankind for ever. 'To live is to change, and to be perfect is to have changed often,' said John Henry Newman, that arch-conservative innovator.[1] But the great Collect in the Book of Common Prayer asks God to free us from the flux to which we are subject – 'That we, who are wearied by the changes and chances of this fleeting world, may rest in thy eternal changelessness'.

The question of the relationship between tradition and innovation is no less acute for the other monotheistic faiths. Our brothers and sisters in Islam and in Judaism are not spared the tensions between the past and the future that feature so much in Christian discourse. But there is a creative tension at the heart of our faith which means that Christianity is, by definition, dynamic. As well as the defining event of the person and saving acts of Jesus, we believe in the continual and constant inspiration of the Holy Spirit as part of the co-eternal Trinity that is God – the Holy Spirit which was poured out upon the first

---

1 John Henry Newman, *An Essay on the Development of Christian Doctrine*, 1.1.7.

disciples and has constantly renewed and invigorated the church ever since. Our faith is based both on an event in history, which happened at a certain time and in a certain place and involved certain people, and on the continually changing and developing relationship we have with the Holy Spirit who leads us into all truth and who intercedes for us with sighs too deep for words. 'I am about to do a new thing' says God in the prophet Isaiah; 'Now it springs forth, do you not perceive it?' (Isaiah 43.19). Or, says the writer of the Gospel of Matthew, 'Therefore every scribe who has been trained for the kingdom of heaven is like the master of a household who brings out of his treasure what is new and what is old.' (Matthew 13.52).

We are drawn forwards. The Judaeo-Christian understanding of humanity made in the image of God and of the perfectibility of human nature affirms our desire – our human need – to understand. In its turn that draws us into new and unknown areas of knowledge and experience. But at the same time we look backwards – we are defined by where we come from, by our history and our memories, by the places we have carved out in our society and communities. The constant challenge is to discern which new things are of the Holy Spirit, and lead us into truth, and which are not. The dialogues and arguments that take place within and between denominations, churches and Christian communities are almost always related to the fundamental questions of the place of authority and revelation in Christian tradition, and the question of whether a change or a revision of practice or doctrine is an elucidation or a denial of the gospel.

Within the New Testament, that process is already apparent. Why do we have four Gospels? Because there were already, before the Gospels were written, a variety of interpretations of Christ's mission and ministry. The Jesus of the Gospel of Mark, written in around 70 CE, is very different from that of the Gospel of John in around 110 CE. Why are there so many Epistles? Because the early church is constantly encountering situations that require a response, that require development of the faith in ways in which it has not had to develop before. For example, the account of the Council of Jerusalem described in Acts 15 and by Paul in Galatians 2. The Council, which wrestled for a long time over the question of whether the followers of Jesus should be required to follow the Jewish law, the Torah, resulted in a solution that both affirmed the tradition (by saying that Jewish people had to continue to observe the law) and shattered it (by saying that Gentiles did not). 'When James and Cephas and John, who were acknowledged pillars, recognized the grace that had been given to me, they gave to Barnabas and me the right hand of fellowship, agreeing that we should go to the Gentiles and they to the circumcised' (Galatians 2.9).

Orthodoxy versus heresy; East versus West; Catholic versus Protestant; Pentecostal versus the rest. In every controversy neither tradition nor innovation has been allowed automatic victory. Marcion, condemned by the early church as a heretic, appealed to scripture and to the saving grace of Jesus Christ to justify his assertion that the Old Testament was inspired by an inferior God. Tertullian, in his response (*Against Marcion*, iv.1–5) insists upon the apostolic authorship of the four Gospels as the source of their authority. Marcion was already, only 100 years after Christ's life, attempting to rediscover the 'authentic' Christ, believing it had become lost in later accretions. Tertullian, the great adversary of heresy (until his break with Christianity in 204 CE) innovates. He introduced the word 'Trinitas' to Christian vocabulary,[2] and in his struggles with his opponents, like Paul, he was passionately seeking ways to interpret the message of Christ for ordinary people in the ordinary places in which they lived and worked.

The Church of England and its fellow churches in the Anglican Communion around the world are, because of their history, right in the middle of this dynamic tension between reform and continuity. The Church of England is both catholic and reformed, goes the catchphrase, but what does that mean? It is in the conjunction of those two words that lie the seeds of conflict down the centuries. The church was created by Henry

---

2 Theophilius, *To Autolycus* 115–181.

VIII. Historians tell us that its creation was partly as a result of a pan-European power struggle involving Spain and Rome, and that it was not the intention of the original founders to forsake all the theological insights of Roman Catholicism any more than they sought slavishly to imitate Rome while rejecting the Pope's authority. Edward VI, Henry's successor, was Protestant; Mary was Catholic. The attempts by both to impose their own versions of Christianity on the nation led to harsh reforms and resulted in many deaths. Elizabeth I, seeking to end the violence that seemed to go hand in hand with religious practice, deliberately sought a middle way between the Catholic Church and the Reformed churches in Europe, but passionate and often violent religious controversy between the different traditions continued throughout the seventeenth century, and its legacy remains with us today.

It is because of this controversy that the Anglican Communion and the Church of England are the strange, unique, hybrid and hard-to-define institutions that they are. One of the greatest minds in Anglican thought, Richard Hooker, was engaged for most of his life in determined argument both with the Reformed tradition and with the Catholic. *The Laws of Ecclesiastical Polity* (1594–1662) was written in part as an extended defence of the Anglican way, and one of the reasons the position of Hooker (and of the Church of England) is often difficult to define is because the controversies in which he was engaged led him to a theology which both combines and synthesizes the sources from which our doctrines and practice spring.

The challenge that confronts the church now, and has always confronted it, is to decide which innovations are in accordance with the gospel and which are not. The Preface of the 1662 edition of the Book of Common Prayer opens: 'It hath been the wisdom of the Church of England ever since the compiling of her publick Liturgy, to keep the mean between the two extremes, of too much stiffness in refusing, and of too much easiness in admitting any variation from it.' But the difficulty of deciding which proposed variations are acceptable and which are not is acknowledged by the compilers: 'and therefore of the sundry alterations proposed to us, we have rejected all such as were of dangerous consequence (as secretly striking at some established doctrine, or laudable practice of the Church of England, or indeed of the whole Catholick Church of Christ) or else of no consequence at all, being utterly frivolous and vain. But such alterations as were tendered to us ... as seemed to us in any degree requisite or expedient, we have willingly ... entered into.'[3] The challenge for us, as for them, is to discern which alterations are 'of dangerous consequence' and which are 'requisite or expedient'; which changes will enable us better to preach the gospel and which would be actively harmful.

* * *

Few churches start with a clean page or a blank slate. By definition, the parish church is serving a community that has often been there for centuries, and even where a community is new it forms part of an older parish and brings its own history and expectations. At the heart of the Church of England's witness is the humdrum daily round of parish life, the Sunday liturgy, the cycle of daily and weekly prayer and worship, pastoral care, evangelism and mission.

But the parish church is a very great deal more than that. Traditionally, and until very recently, it symbolized (alongside the pub and the village green) the community's beating heart. It was the repository for memories and for history, for things that went to make up the community's self-understanding and provided it with a source of commonality and shared experience. It was also, for local families, a place of safety in crisis or death, and a place of celebration of new births, marriages and other rites of passage.

St Peter's Walworth even now is a place of significance to many families who have long since left the area; 'That's the church where Nan got married/where I was baptized/where I had the children done/where we came to for school services.

---

3 Preface, Book of Common Prayer, 1662.

That's where Uncle died when the bomb exploded in the crypt.'
Even now, when the church is much more on the margins, memories and associations run deep and far beyond the community
of regular worshippers, and newcomers quickly learn and assimilate shared history.

'The doctrine or established practice of the Church of England' carries a heavy weight of expectation and demand – of
desire for continuity. Resistance to change is rarely simply a
mischievous piece of meddling by a confused, ill-informed or
NIMBY-ish group of people; it often reflects and is an expression of deep fears and concerns about a perceived path and
possible breaches in the relationship between the past and the
future – resistance to something which may be 'of dangerous
consequence'.

'The sacred', says the English philosopher Roger Scruton, 'is
a human universal.'[4] For many, even in the present secular time,
the parish church continues to be the source and wellspring of
the experience of the sacred. Whether at occasional services like
Remembrance or Harvest or regularly on a Sunday morning or
during the week, many people come to their church hoping to
come closer to and reach a deeper understanding of the God
they worship. The liturgy is not repetitive by accident. Even relatively informal services quickly find a structure that is recog-
nizable and repeated. It helps worshippers to be able to be open
to God if they know where they are. Worship is not carried out
in isolation; it carries within it and is informed by many aspects
of faith and life, of private morality and public ethics, of the
individual as part of a family and the family's relationship with
society; in short, of those things that go to make up the identity
of a person, a family or a community.

My beliefs define who I am, how I find my place in the world,
who and what I perceive other people to be. 'Lord God,' wrote
St Augustine, 'you made us for yourself, and our hearts are rest-
less until they find their rest in you.'[5] Faith, once discovered or

---

4 *Prospect*, July 2007.
5 St Augustine of Hippo, *Confessions*, Book 1.

acknowledged, becomes fundamental. Religious affiliation is, for active members of faith communities, far more than a box ticked on a census form or an occasional source of strength in times of trial or crisis. Beliefs run deep. The decisions people make and the beliefs they hold are in part responses to the world around them – responses that involve a complex combination of factors, from a desire to affirm membership of a community to a desire to neutralize the doubts and fears associated with the vastness of the universe.

Under this weight of expectation, it is not surprising that religions resist change. Religion – literally, the ties that bind – is the communal activity that both responds to and creates the awareness of the sacred. It finds its life in the particular communal practices and rituals that enable people to give expression to the relationship between the mystical other and the concrete world around them. It opens up the community to the sacred through prayer and ritual. Religion is where the mundane and the sacred meet – 'Tread softly, for you tread on my dreams.'[6]

Conversely, it is because the sacred is a human universal (in however many ways it is expressed), and because the church holds such a profound part in the life of many people that change is not just likely but vital. Unless a tradition is renewed, it dies. Plain repetition leads only to further repetition, until the original drama and conception is lost and nothing remains except the husk of a vision, the desiccated bones of a once-vibrant body. Even traditions that are predicated on repetition – long-running plays, political rituals – require new actors and new visions to keep them alive. Historic buildings find new and different functions; places of community reflect and respond to changes in that community, or they lose, very quickly, the significance they have. Societies adapt and change to survive. The Spirit leads us into truth.

A Muslim friend of mine recently surprised me by saying that he is impressed by the way in which the Church of England responds to new discoveries and changes in society. Its reputation

---

6 W. B. Yeats, 'He wishes for the cloths of heaven'.

is for mild-mannered, fence-sitting, unrevolutionary politeness, and it feels counter-intuitive to describe it as having a strong strain of innovation. But in fact there are a great many examples of changes in the church's teaching and practice that have received wide acceptance in spite of initial controversy. Things that seem minor now – candles on the altar, for example – caused people to go to jail in the nineteenth century. Permitting the use of contraception within marriage was hugely controversial when first suggested. The arguments over the ordination of women to the priesthood are fresh in the mind of the church. Few Christians initially supported the abolition of the slave trade.

The process of creating and developing its public liturgy is a very clear example of the way in which the relationship between old and new enables the church to move forward; the 1662 Prayer Book was a revision of the 1549 and 1552 books, and in its turn it has been revised, departed from and then returned to in Order 2 of Common Worship, which itself lies alongside Order 1, the revision of the new liturgies of Series 1, 2, 3 and the Alternative Service Book. There has, over the centuries, been a complex process of change that involves the new and yet is respectful of the past.

* * *

Into this tangled web of expectations and hopes, of resistance and fear, comes the minister or congregation member who wants to draw their congregation into a new place. A place of acceptance, perhaps, or a place that dares to conform more to the gospel values of welcome and openness than it has in the past. A place that is inclusive, in the deepest sense of the word. How can that happen in a way that is true to the way of grace and love to which we are called?

Churches are presented either consciously or unconsciously with a dilemma. If they are to be open, changes will happen. Shadowing the idea of change is risk; for change can be for the worse as well as for the better. Behind risk lies growth, but behind risk lies also fear. There can be great anxiety, which is often about real possibilities – potential loss of identity, for example, or loss of numbers. Perhaps, beneath these fears, is a more fundamental anxiety about becoming the focus of God's disapproval and anger, just as the people of Judah under Ezra and Nehemiah thought they were the recipients of God's anger.

Every parish is different, and each church has its own experience. In the life of St Peter's, five factors were crucial in enabling the church to move on. First, time. Then clarity, confidence and continuity. And finally a recognition and an acceptance that, regrettably but as part of the process, some would leave (and a trust that some would join).

Time is of the essence. But not speed; not rushing to make changes. I was told, before my induction, that it takes five years to turn a parish round. It seems to me that the figure is probably closer to ten. To gain grass roots support for a new vision takes several years and often means that new people must take up roles of responsibility as churchwardens, as members of the church council, as people in training for ministry. For the vision to become part of the lifeblood of the community, to become part of the unconscious day-to-day being of the church, takes longer. Over the ordination of women to the priesthood, for instance, St Peter's had a fairly standard trajectory; from resistance twenty years ago through a grudging recognition five years later (after the departure of several key people to a more conservative church up the road), leading to a passive acceptance five years after that and, ten years later, to the wholehearted indifference which we now enjoy. Indifference as a positive, because the gender of the clergy is rarely a matter of comment, except occasionally and with pleasure – such as when a priest pregnant with twins celebrated the Eucharist on Mothering Sunday. Result, happiness; but the time it's taken has been notable.

Second, clarity. It does a congregation few favours if the leaders are not open and up-front about their vision for the place and how they hope it will be achieved. Any number of Parish Planning Days and Vision Workshops and pieces of flipchart paper stuck around the church with 'Our Hopes for the Future' written on them in wonky handwriting will have little effect unless there comes, from the heart of the church, an honest communication of the challenges and opportunities that lie ahead. Which is not to say that decisions and strategies should be top-down and imposed; rather, that the essence of leadership is in enabling, and people are rarely enabled if they are confused. Clarity of vision can create uncomfortable dynamics, but uncomfortable dynamics can be resolved. Secrecy and unclarity can lead much more easily to misunderstandings and fears; and hard on the heels of that comes the stasis of fear, rabbits hunkering down and hiding for fear of the swoop of the hawk. But clarity of vision and of purpose – 'let me describe the kind of church we might become' – can draw together a congregation in a way that is exciting and inspiring, and can lead it onward into a new and unexpected sense of itself and of its mission.

Third, confidence. The gospel message of God's unconditional love for God's people is not a source of shame. The saving event of the life, death and resurrection of Jesus for all people, everywhere, is a thing most wonderful. The love of God for the world is a message to be proclaimed loudly and clearly. But, and herein lies the paradox, hard on the heels of the proclamation of the gospel message come a whole series of questions about how we live it out in the parish context: a recognition that the world and our daily life is very far from the ideals of the kingdom and that in all things we adjust and compromise, acknowledging the concerns of others and listening to them at the same time as trying to forge a path that approximates to the path of love. Sometimes – often – compromise is necessary; a slowing down, perhaps. Compromise need not be a sign of weakness; it can, rather, be a confident and creative way of acknowledging concerns, a living out of the truth that God loves those who hold diametrically different views to us, and a sign of trust that in the end, after time and with prayer, God's way will become our way. Compromise, as part of a way forward, is important – it acknowledges concerns and anxieties and shows that they are being heard. It holds people in. It is a sign of wanting to include. But compromise requires confidence to be effective.

Fourth, continuity. Lying close alongside the realization that we have time is the fact of our history. It is not possible to understand the Christian message, or the Anglican way, in isolation from the way in which it has come down to us. In a very immediate sense, the recent life of the parish is part of that journey, and within it is much that the church congregation holds to be important – often for strange reasons. At St Peter's we have the habit of turning to face the cross as the clergy and servers process out at the end of the service. We pirouette neatly in our pews. I was told that the reason for this is that it is not right to turn your back on the cross. But in fact it is because, at one point in the distant past, the dismissal at the end of the service was from the back of church. The dismissal is now from the front, but the turning continues, and has, endearingly, become part of our common life. Continuity in the midst of change; both matter. Sheila Saunders, quoted at the beginning of this chapter, acknowledged the continuity – 'When the place opened up, a few years ago, it was like clean water going into a pond. Filling it up with clean water so all the stagnant bits got washed away. The tradition hasn't changed but the cobwebs have been dusted off.' There are good parts of every tradition, in every church, things to preserve and things to celebrate, and part of the way in which support is gained for a new vision is through recognizing, affirming and building on the strengths of the old.

Finally, the recognition that people may leave. Some for good reasons, some for bad. Some because they have been, whether consciously or unconsciously, waiting for a reason – 'I didn't like the way he nudged me to turn the page.' Some because they cannot countenance or have not understood the way in which the congregation is moving – 'There were more of them than there were of us.' Some because they are not being fed any more by what is on offer – 'You don't have a statue of Our Lady.' Especially in the context of a church trying to be inclusive and open, it's regrettable to lose people, particularly from a parish church that should, in an ideal world, offer a place of spiritual and practical welcome to everyone in the parish of whatever faith. But it's also true that it is exactly in the breadth and diversity of the Church of England that our strength lies; realistically, no church can meet all needs. It's true too that for every person who leaves there may well be someone else who thrives; maybe even two people who thrive. It helps, at times, to acknowledge that. The conflict facing the Anglican Communion is partly a conflict about who might leave and who might stay, a conflict that has not yet been resolved. An expectation that losses will occur is, although sad, more liberating than an attempt to bring about change without offending anyone.

I have never been comfortable with the hymn 'Abide with me'. 'Change, and decay, in all around I see; O, thou who changest not, abide with me.' Change and decay are not synonymous. 'I am about to do a new thing. Now it springs forth. Do you not perceive it?' (Isaiah 43.19).

3

The Inclusive Imperative

Susie is of Ghanaian and Jewish parentage. She grew up in Ghana and moved to the UK when she was in her early teens. Via a series of family connections and partly in response to the illness of her baby son, she started coming to St Peter's about five years ago. A Muslim cousin from Ghana was staying with her one summer, and Susie plucked up the courage to invite her to church.

The Gospel reading for that day happened to be the story of the Good Samaritan. A member of the clergy team was preaching. Her reflections on the story had led her to want to retell it in a contemporary setting. Further reflection had led her to the conclusion that, for a congregation in South London at the beginning of the twenty-first century, there was a real parallel in the relation between Islam and Christianity to the relationship between the Jews and the Samaritans in Judah in the first century. The general perception of Islam now is in many ways similar to the fear and disdain in which many Jewish people held Samaritans then.

Louise stood at the front, behind the lectern. 'A man fell among a group of muggers', she said, 'and was beaten and left for dead on the Walworth Road. A priest went past, but looked away as she was late for Evening Prayer. A church-warden went past but was in a rush and moved on. And then, as evening drew in and it started to rain, a Muslim woman in a hijab stopped. She bent over the man, and saw that he was wounded and bleeding. She picked him up, and went across the road to the cab hire place. At first, no one would come out to him, but eventually a Nigerian driver agreed to pick him up and take him to hospital. She went with him, and made sure that he received the attention he needed.'

At the end of the service during the notices, Susie stood up. She introduced her cousin to the congregation and said that her cousin was deeply moved by the whole service, but especially by the sermon. She had, she said, been very anxious about coming to a church; Susie had said it would be OK but she wasn't at all sure. But in the sermon she had heard, for the first time from a Christian leader, a recognition that Muslims are welcome too; that the Christian gospel is a gospel that acknowledges that Muslims too are children of God: and that the love of God is a love that includes Muslims, Christians, Jews and people of all religions and none.

Reflecting afterwards we were struck by how much was being risked in that episode. The risk of replacing Samaritan with Muslim and updating the story, with all the new rawness that that brings with it. The risk Susie was taking by inviting her cousin to church. And the risk Fatimah was taking by coming. But, we thought, that's what inclusion's about. It's about taking risks.

The church exists not for its own sake or even for the sake of its members. It exists for the sake of the world and its liberation. Any dispassionate observer might say that a good place to begin the search for liberation might be with the church itself.[1]

One of the difficulties that faces the church in the early twenty-first century is the disjunction between image and reality. There can be little doubt that the public image of the church to those who are not involved in its daily life is one of conservative inac-

---

1 Keith Ward, *Rethinking Christianity*, 228.

cessibility, a positive lack of welcome to minorities, and generally a sort of self-regarding, backward-looking complacency that is leading the church into inexorable decline.

Close involvement with any number of churches across the country tells a radically different story. Immense efforts are made to be open, welcoming, caring and prayerful. Lively engagement from a bewilderingly wide cross-section of the population means that churches are supporting and engaged in an astonishing range of activities from high-level local political involvement to tiny, struggling mums and toddlers groups; from commissioning art from top-notch contemporary artists to offering care and support to the most vulnerable and marginal members of society. It's true, but bears repeating, that the Church of England has a presence in every community in the land – a remarkable thing after what is generally believed to be 150 years of continuous decline.

Added to that is the fact that many church communities – not all, but many – have a far more diverse and more representative group of members than most other institutions in the area. In terms of income spread, ethnicity, family structures, interests and politics, the sheer breadth of a congregation's makeup can scarcely be matched by other local institutions. Shops, pubs, clubs and membership organizations tend to select or self-select through criteria (wealth, age, interests, political leanings) that result in a narrower and more clearly defined group of stakeholders, members or supporters. Even supermarkets have clearly defined clientele.

Clearly, the criterion of faith allegiance is a limiting factor on the diversity of congregations. But beyond that, the ability of churches to attract and engage such breadth of support is something that should be a cause of celebration and delight, because it demonstrates very clearly that local churches are trying to serve their local communities and communicate a gospel of love and generosity.

Why, then, is this story of good news not recognized and acknowledged by those who have little involvement in the life and work of the church? If Keith Ward's assertion is true, that the church exists not for its own sake but for the sake of the world and its liberation (which echoes William Temple's famous saying that 'The church is the only society on earth which exists for the benefit of non-members'), why are the strides that we have made, towards welcoming and involving local communities in so many and various ways, not more celebrated?

There are many reasons to do with the way the media work and the way in which quiet stories of good news are rarely noticed; to do with the way in which large institutions are no longer trusted as they may have been 50 years ago and with the way in which religion itself is now often seen not as a force for good but as a sign of weakness – external factors to which the church has in some ways contributed but that have also been outside its control.

But there is one area in which we bear a grave proportion of responsibility for the lack of affection in which the churches are now held. We have, certainly, failed to communicate to communities at large that the inclusion that is now largely accepted, and has become second nature in secular society, is also fundamental to Christianity.

Inclusion is not an optional extra. It's not an add-on to the gospel that can be downloaded and installed on a Christian hard drive to make someone's faith more acceptable to the liberal ascendancy. It is an out-working of the implications of God's love for God's world, and a recognition of the profound goodness and beauty of the whole of creation. Inclusion is the acknowledgement that all are equal before God. All are equally loved. An inclusive gospel is a gospel that acknowledges, openly and without restraint, that all are called to receive God's love, and that the external factors that may have caused them to be rejected by others are without validity before the altar. Women, poor people, lesbians, gay people, black people, those with learning difficulties and straight, white, married men are all equal in the eyes of God. All are invited to receive the redemptive love promised and offered by Jesus Christ through his saving act of death and resurrection; in the words of Archbishop Desmond Tutu, 'Christ, when he was lifted up, did not say "I draw some people to myself." He said, "I draw all! All! All!"[2]

The Statement of Belief of the organization Inclusive Church reads:

> We affirm that the Church's mission, in obedience to Holy Scripture, is to proclaim the Gospel of Jesus Christ in every generation.
>
> We acknowledge that this is Good News for people regardless of their sex, race or sexual orientation.
>
> We believe that, in order to strengthen the Gospel's proclamation of justice to the world, and for the greater glory of God, the Church's own common life must be justly ordered.
>
> To that end, we call on our Church to live out the promise of the Gospel; to celebrate the diverse gifts of all members of the body of Christ; and in the ordering of our common life to open the ministries of deacon, priest and bishop to those so called to serve by God, regardless of their sex, race or sexual orientation.[3]

Inclusion, then, at its simplest, is the affirmation that the gospel of Jesus Christ is good news for all people regardless of their gender, ethnicity or sexual orientation. It is the overcoming of the different but connected ways in which the good news has been denied to people through the different but connected forms of historic oppression and exclusion. It is, as the notoriously atheist philosopher Nietzsche realized, 'Christian dynamite'.

> 'Equality of souls before God': this falsehood, this pretext for the rancune [rancour] of all base-minded, this explosive concept which finally became revolution, modern idea and principle of the decline of the entire social order – is Christian dynamite.[4]

---

2 As for example at Chicago in a speech in aid of Lawrence Hall Youth Services, 25 March 2003.
3 www.inclusivechurch.net
4 Friedrich Nietzsche, *The Antichrist*.

Christian dynamite – a combination of words not often applied to Anglican theology, but fundamental to it. Two of the formative episodes in the history of the Church of England – the Elizabethan Settlement and the abolition of the slave trade – were reflections of the comprehensiveness of the gospel that now finds its expression in the deep desire that the church should be truly inclusive. Elizabeth wished to bring to an end the tragic and murderous religious disputes that had taken place in the reigns of her predecessors and to that end she, famously, 'did not wish to make windows into men's souls'. William Wilberforce was motivated by the recognition that the slave trade was not simply unjust, it was inhuman; it denied the fundamental truth that all are equal in the eyes of God and that a just world should reflect that. But the church has allowed its revolutionary gospel to be dried out and distorted, and the radically open message of Jesus Christ has become indistinct and misunderstood.

The call, now, is to make what is de facto de jure; to equip the Anglican Communion with the theological tools to communicate, unashamedly and confidently, the gospel message that *all* are welcome at the altar. But how is this to be done? A meeting in 2005 of the Executive Committee of Inclusive Church looked at developing a theology of inclusion that could be issued as a standard statement of our theological position. One person was invited to present a paper as an opening for discussion; the Committee was expecting swift agreement so that it could move on to the next item.

It quickly became apparent that the 11 people in the room each came at the idea of inclusion from a slightly different standpoint; one, because it reflects the Catholic tradition of breadth and openness, one, because it is a profound statement of the imperative for justice found throughout the Old Testament, one, because it is an expression of the liberal, broad church Anglican tradition. Shot through as the Christian faith and gospel is with the idea, there was no consensus on one particular theological grounding for it.

But if inclusion is, as Giles Fraser says, 'fundamental to the nature of God and at the very heart of the mission and ministry of our Lord Jesus Christ',[5] then we have a responsibility to offer a systematic explanation for it in terms of Christian theology. To root it not in the passing fashions of a swiftly changing world, and not in the political preferences of a group of commentators in mainly western media, but in the heart and core of our faith; in scripture and in doctrine as it has been received and passed on by the Church of England.

Two recent books engage profoundly in the theology of inclusion from an Anglican background. *The Inclusive God* by Steven Shakespeare and Hugh Rayment-Pickard is subtitled 'Reclaiming theology for an inclusive church' and seeks to do just that. *Rethinking Christianity* by Keith Ward takes a more systematic approach. Both offer a developed theology which is open to change and, because of that, thoroughly orthodox – which recognizes the doctrinal core of Christianity as expressed in the creeds and the 'historic formularies of the Church of England' without refusing the lessons and insights that have been uncovered since then – from the great continental theologians such as Kierkegaard, Schleiermacher and Hegel and from the British tradition as represented by Hooker and his successors. But there is more; the insights of liberation theology, queer and feminist theology and theology from non-western countries (especially from Asia) have brought depth and vision to the interpretation of the gospel that says, loudly and clearly, that no one can be left out from the kingdom of God for which we are all called to work.

According to the authors of *The Inclusive God*, an inclusive theology is

> A theology in which doctrine is never divided from living, questioning wonder, nor from an ethical commitment to the full human dignity of each person. Nothing less than this is what it means to *start with creation*.[6]

---

5 Giles Fraser in Steven Shakespeare and Hugh Rayment-Pickard, *The Inclusive God*, Foreword.

6 Steven Shakespeare and Hugh Rayment-Pickard, *The Inclusive God*, 22, emphasis added.

The great poem that opens the book of Genesis, the first creation story, is generally agreed to have been written in Babylon after the fall of Jerusalem during the Exile. It was a time of calamity, when it seemed that the Promised Land had been taken away, and the relationship between Yahweh and Yahweh's chosen people had been broken – a time of self-searching and questioning, when the very basis of the faith they held was undermined. But the poem repeats, not once but many times, the confident affirmation: 'And God saw that it was good.' The light is good, the Earth is good, the seas are good, the vegetation is good; 'God saw everything that he had made, and indeed, it was very good.' In the middle of this confident affirmation of the goodness of creation – unusual in creation myths – comes the unequivocal celebration of the creation of humanity.

So God created humankind in his image. In the image of God he created them; male and female he created them.
Genesis 1.27

This is the starting point of a theology of inclusion. For if each of us is made in the image of God, male and female, wherever we originate, whatever our attributes, our skills, our wisdom or our gender, then each of us is to be welcomed, not in spite of what we are but because of who we are – created in the image of God.

God's question to a recently dead soul comes to mind – 'Did you enjoy my creation?' Inclusion is about celebration, and about the belief that the cosmos was made in love, by love and for love. As human beings we are invited to participate in the constant act of God's creation, and to challenge all that stands in the way of life and love. The opening words of the Nicene Creed identify the context for the Christian faith – 'I believe in God the Father Almighty, creator of heaven and earth, and of all things visible and invisible.'

If the rest of the Hebrew Scriptures were as unequivocal as the opening of Genesis might lead us to hope, the task of explaining an inclusive theology would be a great deal simpler. But it all goes wrong very quickly. The story of the forbidden fruit, of Adam and Eve, represents in archetype the story of humanity, seeking greater understanding (the tree of the knowledge of good and evil) but in the process discovering its own separation from God. Finding knowledge but also discovering difference. The story of the casting out of Adam and Eve from the garden is a graphic description of the consequences of the human desire for knowledge and identity; 'Then the eyes of both were opened, and they knew that they were naked; and they sewed fig leaves together and made loincloths for themselves' (Genesis 3.7).

* * *

The challenges that face us now were no less acute for the people of God in the period after the Exile and before the destruction of the temple in 70 CE. They were beset by the same questions and dilemmas that face every community. At their profoundest level, these questions revolve around the tension between the infinite and boundless love of God and a community's need to survive. The tension, in other words, between the unique and the universal.

The stories of the descendants of Adam, of Noah, of Abraham, of Lot, of Isaac and Jacob and of their wives and children are the foundation stories of Judaism and Christianity. There are many themes that run through these stories. A central theme is the identification between the Hebrew people and the Promised Land. 'I will establish my covenant between me and you ... and I will give to you, and to your offspring after you, the land where you are now an alien, all the land of Canaan, for a perpetual holding; and I will be their God' (Genesis 17.7, 8).

The covenantal relationship is referred to explicitly in parts of the Hebrew scriptures, especially those that were written or edited during and after the Exile. But it is sometimes interpreted as a contract, which requires certain kinds of behaviour and marks of identity and sometimes understood as an unconditional relationship between God and God's people. The loss of the land, the Exile, and the way in which the people of God were

conquered and subjugated, is understood by many of the prophets to be evidence that they are not living in accordance with
the covenant and that their religious leaders are responsible;
that they have mixed too much with the people around them;
that they have followed foreign gods and consorted with foreign
women. They have betrayed their identity as the Chosen People,
and therefore they are being punished for their backsliding and
their failure to observe the law.

There is within the Hebrew Scriptures a strand that can,
by any measure, be seen as disturbingly exclusive. The book
of Ezra, for example, written some time after 444 BCE, after
the return of the exiles from Babylon, is insistent that the Jewish people must return to the purity they enjoyed previously in
order to rediscover the favour of God. Chapters 9 and 10 of
Ezra make deeply uncomfortable reading:

> Then Ezra the priest stood up and said to them, 'You have
> trespassed and married foreign women, and so increased the
> guilt of Israel. Now make confession to the LORD the God of
> your ancestors, and do his will; separate yourselves from the
> peoples of the land and from the foreign wives.' Then all the
> assembly answered with a loud voice 'It is so; we must do as
> you have said.' [A long list of those who had married foreign
> women follows.] All these had married foreign women, and
> they sent them away with their children.
> (Ezra 10.10–12, 44)

The purpose of the purity code (the Law) in Leviticus and
Deuteronomy is to enable the people of Israel to live as a single,
separated community, unsullied by the activities of the tribes
and peoples around them. The histories and the prophetic writings are unanimous in their rejection of Baal worship and the
people of Baal so that the integrity and purity of the covenant
people can be preserved.

As contemporary scholarship is uncovering, the reality of the
situation was much more complex. The intermingling of different peoples in Israel and Judah was very considerable. Baal wor-

ship was by no means exclusive to foreigners. The ideal of ethnic purity was not realized, which perhaps explains why the call to walk apart from foreigners and idolatrous people is repeated so often.

The Californian theologian and activist Ched Myers has written on the counterpoint within the Hebrew scriptures between exclusivity and welcome. He reminds us that in spite of the fact that a dominant strand in the Hebrew scriptures seeks to set apart the people of Israel, the strand of generosity and inclusion is equally vital. At Inclusive Church's first birthday celebration in Putney in August 2004, he gave a seminar that has subsequently been developed into 'A House for All Peoples? A Biblical Study on Welcoming the Outsider', published in *Sojourner* magazine in April 2006. He focuses on Third Isaiah – in particular, Isaiah 56.3, 4, 8:

> Do not let the foreigner joined to the LORD say, 'The LORD will surely separate me from his people'; and do not let the eunuch say, 'I am just a dry tree.' For thus says the LORD: To the eunuchs who keep my sabbaths, who choose the things that please me and hold fast my covenant, I will give, in my house and within my walls, a monument and a name better than sons and daughters; I will give them an everlasting name that shall not be cut off ... Thus says the Lord GOD, who gathers the outcasts of Israel, I will gather others to them besides those already gathered.

Scholars generally agree that Third Isaiah was written after the return from Babylon at about the same time Ezra and Nehemiah were constructing the Jewish state after the Exile. But his message, and the message of Second Isaiah, writing during the Exile, is very different –

> Ho, *everyone* who thirsts,
> come to the waters;
> and you that have no money,
> come, buy and eat!
> Isaiah 55.1

The Torah acknowledges that even Israelites are 'but tenants and strangers in the land' –

The land shall not be sold in perpetuity, for the land is mine; with me you are but aliens and tenants.
Leviticus 25.23

In Deuteronomy the Jews are commanded to care for others in their midst –

You shall not withhold the wages of poor and needy labourers, whether other Israelites or aliens who reside in your land in one of your towns. You shall pay them their wages daily before sunset, because they are poor and their livelihood depends on them.
Deuteronomy 24.14, 15

There are many other writings that go beautifully beyond the boundaries of the chosen people's self-identity – the Song of Songs, for example – and others still, especially the Wisdom strand and some of the Psalms, which are explicitly and avowedly universal in their approach – for example, Proverbs 8. The radical nature of the Hebrew belief in God as universal creator was always in tension with the belief that God's chosen people must be set apart by nature of the identity to which God is calling them. Both are vital, but sometimes one is allowed to flourish at the cost of the other. The dynamic tension that exists within every Christian community – the tension between identity and inclusion – is equally present in the Hebrew scriptures.

Just as the creation story underpins the Old Testament, so the incarnation is the ground base of the New, and of all subsequent Christian theology. 'He was conceived by the Holy Spirit, born of the Virgin Mary, and was made man.' As the notion of the goodness of creation is part of the warp and weft of the Hebrew scriptures, so the heart of the Christian story is the belief that in Christ God became human. It is through the full co-inherence of God with humanity in the person of Christ that humanity is brought into full co-inherence with God. Jesus 'emptied himself, taking the form of a slave, being born in human likeness. And being found in human form, he humbled himself, and became obedient to the point of death – even death on a cross' (Philippians 2.7, 8).

If the dominant imperative of the Hebrew scriptures is the need to overcome the separation between God and Israel, symbolized by the loss of the Promised Land because of the failure to observe the Torah, at the heart of the New Testament is the recognition that reconciliation has taken place in the person and saving act of Jesus Christ, the one fully human and fully divine being. Through that reconciliation, *all* have the potential to be brought into the household of God, citizens with the saints and no longer strangers and aliens in the land. The inclusive love of God is made manifest in the life and love of Jesus.

The New Testament has been described as an extended midrash on the Hebrew scriptures. The name 'New Testament' or 'New Covenant' indicates the radical nature of the change that was brought about by Jesus' life and teaching. 'You have heard ... but I say to you.' Again and again, Jesus takes the words of the Hebrew scriptures and reapplies them, and the unprecedented message of the gospel becomes clear. In the Gospel of Luke, Jesus begins his ministry with a reference to the book of the prophet Isaiah – the words are no less powerful because of their familiarity:

> The Spirit of the Lord is upon me, because he has anointed me to bring good news to the poor. He has sent me to proclaim release to the captives and recovery of sight to the blind, to let the oppressed go free, to proclaim the year of the Lord's favour.
> Luke 4.18, 19

Almost a manifesto for the work of Jesus, its radical nature is apparent in its rejection of the purity codes and the holiness codes of Leviticus and Deuteronomy. The writer of Luke goes on to make this plain – Elijah, the greatest prophet 'was sent to none of [the Israelites] except to a widow at Zarepath in Sidon ... And none was cleaned except Naaman the Syrian' (Luke 4.26, 27). Both are from beyond the borders of Israel. It is small wonder that 'all who heard him in the synagogue were filled with rage. They got up, drove him out of the town, and led him to the brow of the hill on which their town was built, so that they might hurl him off the cliff' (Luke 4.28).

Jesus constantly refers to the writings of the law and the prophets, but in ways that subvert their meaning and implications. In the Gospel of Mark, chapters 7 and 8 encapsulate the remarkable expansion and development of Jewish theology that, in the end, leads to the separation of Judaism from Christianity. At the beginning of chapter 7, after the Pharisees have attacked the disciples for eating with unclean hands, Jesus arraigns them for abandoning the commandment of God and holding to human tradition. Verse 14, re-emphasized in verses 20–23, must have sounded astonishingly radical then, as it still does now: 'It is what comes out of a person that defiles. For it is from within, from the human heart, that evil intentions come ... All these evil things come from within, and they defile a person.'

Immediately after that comes the healing of the Syro-Phoenician's daughter, the first miracle in Mark involving a Gentile, which takes place only after Jesus has been bested by the Syro-Phoenician woman in a discussion. Following that comes the second feeding miracle, which is specifically about feeding the Gentiles in the region of the Decapolis. It is not until Jesus' ministry has, clearly and explicitly, moved beyond the people of Israel and into the Gentiles, and beyond the holiness codes of the Hebrew scriptures into the recognition that each person must take responsibility for their own salvation, that Jesus can finally be acknowledged by Peter as 'The Christ, the Son of the Living God.' Peter's confession is the fulcrum of the Gospel of Mark; immediately after it come some of the hardest sayings of Jesus, an acknowledgement that the implications of a faith that seeks to include everyone are very difficult both to understand and to live out.

If there could be any doubt as to the way in which Jesus appropriates the 'open' tradition of Third Isaiah, he refers to it during Luke's account of the cleansing of the temple.

> In the midst of his dramatic 'exorcism' of the temple, Jesus quotes directly from our text: 'My house shall be called a house of prayer for all peoples' (Luke 19:46 parallels Isaiah 56:7). It was this vision of radical inclusion that animated Jesus' constant transgressions of the social boundaries of his day: eating with lepers, hanging out with women, touching the impure, teaching the excluded. More than anything else, it may have been what got him strung up.[7]

In the Gospel of John, the story of the woman at the well demonstrates Jesus' disregard for contemporary boundaries. She is there in the heat of the day – alone – because she has been ostracized by the town. Jesus has no compunction in asking her for water, and then speaks to her with no concern for the differences between them. Far from being afraid and affronted by Jesus' knowledge that she has had five husbands and that the one she has now is not her husband, the Samaritan woman rushes back to town (from where she has been ostracized) and says, 'Come and see a man who told me everything I have ever done! He cannot be the Messiah, can he?' (John 4.29). Her delight is in being recognized for who she is, without condemnation. 'I came', says Jesus in the Gospel of John, 'that they may have life, and have it abundantly' (John 10.10).

The inclusive imperative is finally restated at the end of Matthew's Gospel:

> Go therefore, and make disciples of all nations, baptizing them in the name of the Father and of the Son and of the Holy Spirit, and teaching them to obey everything that I have commanded you.
> Matthew 28.19, 20

---

7 Ched Myers, 'A House for All Peoples?'.

But just as the Hebrew scriptures are complex and hard to understand, and just as there is a dynamic tension between the universality of God's love and the particularity of the Jewish people, so Christian theology does not stop with the incarnation. The crucifixion and the resurrection are the counterpart to the incarnation; the saving event that overcomes the separation between God and humanity through the reconciling love that Christ lives out, even to death.

It is no part of an inclusive theology to deny the reality or the consequences of sin. Fear and loathing are no less present in the world now than they were in the first century of the Christian era, and we constantly struggle to overcome them. But a theology of inclusion, in starting with the creation and the incarnation, is defined by the belief that love comes before fear, and inclusion before rejection. It starts with God's love for the world and God's miraculous in-breaking into the world, and from there it shows us how to undo the tragic separation of humanity from God.

* * *

'Christ is the end of the law.' And yet, the law remains. No one struggles with the relationship between love and the law more than Paul. John Robinson famously called his commentary on the letter to the Romans *Wrestling with Romans*, for the epistle is complex and dense. It is dense because in it Paul is passionately engaged in the task of working out the implications of faith in the saving love of Jesus. For Paul was a Jew, born under the law, and yet he believes that Christ is the end of the law.

The letter to the Galatians contains some of Paul's most succinct arguments about the relationship between those who follow Christ and the law. Writing in the heat of controversy and in deep pain, he is responding to what he has learned about the church in Galatia – that some teachers are saying that the Galatians must seek circumcision and to follow the Jewish law if they are to be true followers of Christ. Paul's response, forged in controversy and written in passion, has become the epicentre of Christian inclusivity:

Now that faith has come, we are no longer subject to a disciplinarian, for in Christ Jesus you are all children of God through faith. As many of you as were baptized into Christ have clothed yourselves with Christ. There is no longer Jew or Greek, there is no longer slave or free, there is no longer male and female; for all of you are one in Christ Jesus. And if you belong to Christ, then you are Abraham's offspring, heirs according to the promise.
Galatians 3.25–29

Familiarity with this passage perhaps dulls the radical nature of its meaning. It is the outworking of the belief that whoever is in Christ is a new creation. A new creation that brings us all to a new identity, an identity that does not consist in being Greek or Jewish, male or female; we are all made one in the freedom that is the love of God.

For in Christ Jesus neither circumcision nor uncircumcision counts for anything; the only thing that counts is faith working through love.
Galatians 5.6

Paul insists, in the teeth of the opposition of all the leading disciples of Jesus – 'James and Cephas and John, who were acknowledged pillars' – that salvation is by the grace of God and not by observance of the Jewish law. The letter to the Romans reflects his belief that whoever is baptized into Christ is no longer under the law:

Owe no one anything, except to love one another; for the one who loves another has fulfilled the law.
Romans 13.8

The only entry qualification is belief in Christ crucified and resurrected, which brings about the profound freedom in God's love so that structures, customs, biology and everything that defines our human identity falls away. We are all, simply, equally beloved children of God.

Of course, in the writings of Paul no less than in the Hebrew scriptures, the dynamic tensions between the things that enable us to say 'I am', to name ourselves, and the radical freedom of the love of God are emphatically present; the tension between *sarx* (flesh) and *pneuma* (spirit); between this-worldly bodies in which we are still clothed and the other-worldly love into which we are reborn. The life of the Christian community is defined by its behaviour as much as its faith, and for this reason Paul finds that he has to issue guidance and direction to the new communities he is supporting. The consequences of that guidance are with us now; and it is over the writings of St Paul that the greatest disagreements about the nature of the inclusive gospel take place.

I turn to that in the next chapters. But the essential truth that informs the Hebrew scriptures, the Gospels and the letters of St Paul is this: that the transforming love of God is intended for all peoples – Jews and Gentiles, slaves and free, male and female. Each person is created in the image of God, brought close to God through the incarnation, crucifixion and resurrection of Christ, and can through that love be reborn, no longer under the law but in love.

* * *

The church is called to be a place of engagement. A place that inspires, where those who are seeking a more profound expression of spirituality can find refreshment and encouragement; where those who are in pain or are vulnerable can find a place of safety and support; and where those who wish to know and understand God better can move forward down that path. In essence, the church should be a place that receives vulnerability and self-doubt, fear and anxiety, desire and need; and, by grace, enables it to be transformed into something other. A place of abundant love.

That requires a willingness to change, be open and be challenged. And yet, at the same time, it also requires the ability to offer stability and continuity, support and safety. The paradox at the heart of the Hebrew scriptures is the same paradox that faces ordinary churches in England – how do we respond to the radical economy of the love of God while at the same time being, and becoming, the people we are? How do we offer the welcoming and inclusive love of God while at the same time retaining an identity, a sense of self, that enables us to be constant and caring in our relationships with others?

Jesus changed his mind after his encounter with the Syro-Phoenician woman (Mark 7.24). Peter changed his mind after his vision in Joppa (Acts 10.9). Paul changed his mind after his conversion encounter with Christ, described graphically in Acts (Acts 9.1–19) and more mysteriously in the second letter to the Corinthians (2 Corinthians 12.2–4). The inclusive imperative calls us to be willing to change our minds, change our ways of life, and change our perception of who we are. At its best, an inclusive church is one that recognizes at the profoundest level that those who come to it are vulnerable and questioning, and have, in many cases, been damaged or hurt by previous encounters with religion.

'How', Ruth, a member of St Peter's was asked, 'do you cope with the Christian God?' The questioner was perplexed by the difference between Ruth's approach to spirituality and religion and his image of the jealous and exclusive God of Christianity. 'For me,' answered Ruth, 'God is like a washing line.' By which she meant that the more she understands her faith, the more meanings of the word God she discovers. Each one is placed on the washing line where she can see them, all alongside each other. It is a good image for a Christian community, which will probably have as many different conceptions of God as there are people in the community.

If believers were colours, they could be placed on a spectrum as wide as the rainbow. At one end are those who tend more to the Ezra/Nehemiah approach to faith, seeking clarity of definition, clear boundaries to the community, clearly identifiable members and categorical rules for the behaviour and conduct of members. Some are influenced most heavily by the theology of Calvin – others take a fundamentalist approach to the Bible. At the other end are those for whom the community has edges that are so fuzzy that they can scarcely be seen, where membership is fluid, where the word of God is to be heard in strange and unexpected places, where surprises and shocks are as important as continuity and predictability. The 'Sea of Faith' movement towards the end of the last century is one of the best-known manifestations of this kind of faith.

The task of trying to reconcile these two opposites is a task that falls to an inclusive church. If all are made in the image of God, and all are welcome at the altar, then it is as exclusive to make it difficult for those who seek clarity to be members of the community as it is to shut out those who seek something much more undefined.

Doreen is one of the longest-standing members of St Peter's. Originally from Barbados, she has been attending for nearly 20 years. I noticed quite early on in my time at the church that she did not receive communion. After a little time I asked her why. Because, she replied, her mother had been turned away on the steps of the church in the 1960s when she arrived, and Doreen felt it would be wrong to take communion where her mother had been refused it. After a couple of years, she began to take communion in the Lady Chapel, but even now she only takes communion at the main altar on Maundy Thursday and Good Friday.

Toro is Nigerian. She began coming to the church about 15 years ago. After a few years she gave up coming because she felt so unwelcome. Five years later she came back, and has been coming ever since. Her explanation is simple: St Peter's is her parish church and she doesn't see why she shouldn't be able to come here.

These are both examples of where a gospel has been communicated that is not inclusive; a gospel that has made assumptions and assertions on the basis of factors that have nothing to do with the love of God and everything to do with the way society works – the way it welcomes some and does not welcome others, the way some are automatically near the top of the pile and others near the bottom. Where the first shall be first and the last, last.

They are also examples of ways in which the gospel survives the mauling it is given by humanity. Both Doreen and Toro recognized the profound truth that the church is there for them, and they acted on this truth. Doreen continued to come and took communion in the Lady Chapel, celebrating God's love but also respecting the memory of her mother. Toro came back, determined not to be refused a place in the Anglican Church in which she was born and raised back home in Nigeria.

Most churches recognize the principle of being inclusive; of welcoming the stranger, the widow and the orphan, the outsider. Most churches are, in theory, keen to grow and to encourage a wider membership. But if individuals and groups understand why the need to be open is not just a growth strategy but an intrinsic part of the gospel, they are more likely to overcome their all-too-frequent fears of outsiders and strangers, and to recognize God in the common humanity of all people.

'If any want to be my followers, let them deny themselves and take up their cross and follow me' (Mark 8.34). It is in dying to ourselves that we live. An inclusive theology is a theology of death to self, of loss of identity. It is about being cast into the unknown, being taken into exile, into the wilderness – because it is in the wilderness that each person is stripped down, deprived of all that enables them to lord it over others, to shut others out, to oppress the weak and cast out the different.

So churches are invited to be places that offer a way into the wilderness where each person can discover what Christ is calling them to. But for this to happen they must also be places of safety that enable the first steps of trust to be taken, and where those tentative contacts can be made that may, over weeks, months or even years, bear fruit in a radically different self-understanding, a new identity, and a re-imagined membership of the body of Christ.

The Christian community is built through meetings and encounters, casual conversations, arguments, prayer and laughter. The insistence by Doreen and Toro that they would not be excluded from the church had to be matched by the recognition within the existing congregation that their (implicit) self-identity – as a white church that had little space for black people – was open to challenge. Stasis is never achieved, but neither is it ever in total flux. A healthy Christian community is a dynamic thing, which never rests where it is, is always moving on, and yet never forgets the story of its birth and the roots from which it came. But at the heart of it all is the radically inclusive notion of the equality of souls before God – Christian dynamite.

4

Remove Packaging Before Use

Jason Maldonado:
'The thing about our civil partnership service was that there were loads of people there who had never been so welcomed. For many of them it was the first time in an Anglican church, but they all said it just felt "normal". More people were surprised that we had champagne in church afterwards than by the service. Because Chris and I were giving out the communion wine, it was as if we were welcoming them to our home.

'I grew up in the Bronx and was the seventh of 14 children. My Mum was Catholic and my Dad Pentecostal. They couldn't agree on which church to go to so they decided to raise us Lutheran. We practically lived in the church when I was a kid – I remember playing there, eating the wafers and drinking out of the shot glasses they had for communion. But in 1987 my Mum and I were caught in a shoot-out, and my parents decided to move to rural Virginia. I started going to a Methodist youth club, which was lots of fun – seeing ghosts in the churchyard, you know the kind of thing. Friendship. But I was coming to terms with my sexuality, and when I was 14 a 19-year-old volunteer came out as a gay man to the church. He and his family stopped going because of the reaction. I could see that would happen to us so I left. Then I tried the Mormons too, which was much more wild but no one talked about it, but I didn't feel as though I belonged there. I went to a Methodist college where

*you got extra credits for going to chapel, but while I was
there I decided I couldn't hide my sexuality any longer and
came out. It was the talk of the college, but quite quickly I
got the "We are right, you are wrong, you're gonna go to hell"
treatment.*

*'So in the end I transferred to Washington. I didn't go to
church for a year – I discovered the more "obvious" side of gay
life. My grades suffered and after a bit they said I should take
a semester out. I realized I needed to get my life together.*

'Basically I was searching, and searching, and searching.

*'Somebody told me about a service for gay and lesbian
Catholics called Dignity. I decided to go. I drove round the
block five times before going in. Then, when I finally went, it
was a commitment blessing. I just cried, and cried. I slipped
out at the end; it was all too much. I didn't go back for six
months but after that I didn't miss a Dignity mass for three
years. It was the first time I'd seen loads of people, together,
who were OK with being gay. I belonged there.*

*'When I moved to England to be with Chris, we agreed that
we had to find a church to go to. I did a trawl on the internet
and found a branch of Dignity meeting in Essex. On our way
there our first Sunday, Chris said, "Why don't we just go to
the parish church?" I said there was absolutely no way I was
going there. It would be full of a bunch of bigots and I was
certainly not going back into the closet. We had a huge row
all the way to the bus stop but Chris won and we went in.
The people inside looked like the kind of people who would
be conservative – scrubbed faces and smart clothes. I sat and
glowered right through the service, and then at the end another clergy person got up in the Notices and started saying
to everyone that they had to go to a Mass near Lambeth Palace that week and pray that the Primates (who were meeting there) would start making the Anglican Communion a
genuinely welcoming place for gay and lesbian Christians.*

'"Oh My God!" I thought.

'And now we're at home. As soon as we arrived everyone wanted to tell us about their gay best friend. At St Peter's I was, quickly, so much more than "Jason who's gay". I was Jason who has a partner. I was Jason who chats with Shirley walking her dog. I was Jason who read and did Junior Church. It's the closest thing I can imagine to growing up in the Lutheran church. It's a family. It's full circle.

The point about inclusivity is that it's everyday.'

Is our society broken? I think it is. We are in a phase of our culture where the fragmentation of society is far more obvious. It's not just families, it's different ethnic communities and economic groups. We talk about access and equality the whole time, but in practice we all seem to live very segregated lives.[1]

It's a truism that 'we live in a postmodern world'. The word 'postmodern' is used with great frequency, but little clarity, to characterize the way the world is perceived now. Underlying it is the idea that there is no longer a 'metanarrative' – according to the French philosopher Baudrillard, we live in an age of 'simulacra and simulation ... in which there is no longer any God to recognize his own, nor any last judgment to separate true from false, the real from its artificial resurrection'.[2] The narrative that until recently largely defined a person's identity, status and faith was a shared narrative. My parents' generation had an understanding of history bound up with ideas about empire, God and nation; a common context shared with friends, family and colleagues that enabled a conversation to take place without the need for complicated mutual enlightenment and explanation.

The situation now is far more complex. To an extent unimaginable before the advent of mass transport and mass individual communication (the internet instead of terrestrial TV),

---

1 Archbishop Rowan Williams, *Daily Telegraph*, 15.9.2007.
2 Jean Baudrillard, 'The Evil Demon of Images'.

communities of geography – villages, towns, neighbourhoods –
have given way to communities of engagement, where links are
no longer dependent on face-to-face contact and shared local
activities but on shared interests and shared concerns, varying
from website forums on the best way to bring up children to
fascination with any number of conspiracy theories to communities of music to idiosyncratic kinds of sport or sexual involvement. 'Friendship' is no longer necessarily a relationship created
and developed through regular physical meetings – the advent
of Facebook and MySpace have put paid to that – and the differences between and within generations and ethnic groups, instead of becoming smaller are far greater than they were in the
1950s.

As a result, we have become highly skilled semiologists, developing our ability to identify and categorize people whom we
encounter according to a number of different factors, not all immediately obvious. For instance, in the UK accents are no longer
a reliable reflection of class, and automatic assumptions about
gender-specific roles are, thankfully, a thing of the past. Sociologists and philosophers are deeply engaged in analysis and argument about the reasons for such dramatic changes in society.
Argument too continues on whether the result has been an increase in the sum total of human happiness. But the explosion
of identities is a big part of the challenge that the churches are
now facing. It is most clearly expressed in the range of identities
associated with sexual orientation and gender – gay, lesbian,
bisexual, transsexual, transgendered, intersexed, male, female,
androgynous, butch, femme – but equally in the way in which
newly confident communities request recognition in new ways
– gay pride, black pride, feminist and developing world theology, the Paralympics. It has become very clear that one size no
longer fits all, whether in relation to education, sport, entertain-
ment or faith.

'This is my truth, tell me yours,' say the Manic Street Preachers. Underlying postmodernism is the notion that there is no
notion of absolute truth; that each person has their own truth,
their own understanding of the universe and of their place in it.

The philosopher Wittgenstein recognized that language has no meaning beyond that which is ascribed to it by language, and all ascribed meaning is situationally specific. We use language to say what words mean, and the language used is inextricably bound up with the culture and the situation in which it is used. Twentieth-century philosophy engages constantly with the notion that there can be no universally agreed meaning or truth to which assent can be either requested or expected. A large body of academic opinion holds that our interpretation of phenomena and of experiences is entirely subjective, and although we can try to communicate it and to explain it in a way that receives assent from others, our interpretation has no privilege over that of, say, a fundamentalist Muslim or a militant atheist. The meaning of language is culturally and temporally specific.

But there is another side to this portrayal of contemporary life. For, in spite of all that has been written and observed about the segmentation and segregation of society, it is possible to construct an argument that below the diversity is a very powerful desire for commonality; not just that individuals seek community among those with whom they form links of interest or activity, but that there remains a desire for a wider community, to be part of something greater than themselves. The 'celebrity culture' has received acres of condemnatory newsprint, but far more acres of admiring quasi-hagiography. Common culture demands a commonality of language, and in spite of the eruption of diversity in media and method, the focus of this diversity is relatively narrow. Whichever paper is read, whichever current events website is accessed, the information and the news on it is similar.

In other words, in spite of an expressed desire for individuality, we often pursue conformity. The fashion store, the TV serial, popular culture: conversation around the water cooler in the office depends on shared experience, 'teenagers all sound the same', and despite the apparent diversity of desire, the common currency is one of commonality. The Sunday afternoon trek to the shopping mall; national or international sporting events; TV icons and celebrities; society functions on the basis of mutuality, not individuality, and most people would in the end prefer to conform than to sit out on a limb. The present situation is by no means as black and white as some fear; shared experience – and locality – still matters.

'Pilate asked him, "What is truth?"' (John 18.38). Where are the churches in all of this? What role can we play, those of us who work within a long-established tradition and yet know that our mission is to be responsive to the needs of the new communities we try to serve? The churches are perched, very uncomfortably, on the razor-sharp cusp between the modern and the postmodern. On the one hand, we are part of a long and complicated tradition, derived directly from Jesus and the Gospels and passing down across the centuries through the Fathers, Augustine, Aquinas, the Reformation, the Enlightenment, and the growth and development of the post-Reformation, Protestant and Pentecostal churches. On the other hand, our communities are made up of people who are fairly and squarely part of the twenty-first-century world, both seeking individuation and valuing conformity. Each person brings the breadth of the postmodern world into the depth of the Christian tradition. The challenge with which the churches are faced is to unravel the relationship between continuity and change, so that they can offer nourishment to those who are genuinely seeking a profound understanding of their spirituality and a dynamic relationship with God.

> But speaking the truth in love, we must grow up in every way into him who is the head, into Christ, from whom the whole body, joined and knit together by every ligament with which it is equipped, as each part is working properly, promotes the body's growth in building itself up in love.
> Ephesians 4.15–16

The American writer Andrew Walls, in his essay 'The Ephesian Moment', subtitled 'At a Crossroads in Christian History', reflects on these questions. The letter to the Ephesians is concerned with Christian behaviour and the life of the church at a moment

of crisis in the young church's life. Nearly all the original followers of Jesus were Jewish, and followed Jewish law – observing
ritual purity and spending time in the Temple praising God. As
the story of Christ is told to the Gentiles, many begin to convert.
Initially, the expectation among the followers of Christ in Jerusalem is that new converts will adopt the Jewish laws, circumcision, and purity requirements. But the letter to the Ephesians
takes a different approach.

> For [Christ] is our peace; in his flesh he has made both groups
> into one and has broken down the dividing wall, that is,
> the hostility between us. He has abolished the law with its
> commandments and ordinances, so that he might create in
> himself one new humanity in place of the two, thus making
> peace, and might reconcile both groups to God in one body
> through the cross.
> Ephesians 2.14–16

The Jews and the Gentiles were, in their common faith,
forced to encounter one another. New questions were raised.
Previously the question for Jews of, say, eating food sacrificed to
idols would not have arisen, for they would not have been in situations where such food might be offered. It was a result both of
the Jewish diaspora but more importantly of the close relationship between Jewish and Gentile followers of Christ that these
questions had to be asked; and having been asked, an answer
had to be found.

Those who were Jewish agreed to continue with observing
the law, the Torah – but observance was not required of Gentiles. Therefore the diversity of contemporary culture was recognized and affirmed within the structures of the emergent new
religion.

> Emphatically, there was to be only *one* Christian community
> ... The Ephesian letter is not about cultural homogeneity; cul-
> tural diversity had already been built into the church by the
> decision not to enforce the Torah. It is a celebration of the

union of irreconcilable entities, the breaking down of the wall
of partition, brought about by Christ's death.[3]

What are the implications of that for the church today? The
Anglican Communion is caught up in a major conflict partly
because the dominant voice in Christianity is no longer western. The diversity of Christian communities, across the world,
in Asia, Latin America, the Middle East and Africa, with their
different theological, ethical and ecclesiastical frameworks, is
bringing a series of new questions to the church in England
and in North America. The letter to the Ephesians does not
seek to impose a particular form of unity on the church; on the
contrary, it finds a way to ensure that the differences between
Christians, even those that may seem irreconcilable, can be not
only accommodated but also celebrated.

The Ephesian metaphors of the temple and of the body show
each of the culture-specific segments as necessary to the body
but as incomplete in itself. Only in Christ does completion,
fullness, dwell ... We need each other's vision to correct, enlarge, and focus our own; only together are we complete in
Christ.[4]

An inclusive church is not a homogeneous church. It's not a
'one size fits all'. It's a church that recognizes and respects the
breadth of culture, ways of life, influences and activities of the
people it tries to serve. Each locality is different – some areas
are ethnically homogeneous and contain people from a relatively narrow range of incomes and employment, while others
are wildly diverse and contain people from all over the world
carrying out a range of work from highly paid banking to very
early morning office cleaning and security. But the questions
facing churches are similar – even at a church with a largely
professional, white, middle-class congregation, the congregants

3 Andrew Walls, *Cross-Cultural Process*, 4.
4 Andrew Walls, *Cross-Cultural Process*, 6.

might include children, young people, the elderly, single people, families, financiers, journalists, teachers, the unemployed and retired. There may be Conservatives and Labour voters, musicians and sportspeople, academics and people who haven't opened a book in the last ten years. Each of them seeks nourishment; each of them wishes to be seen, to be recognized, to be understood and to be affirmed. 'We must grow up ... into Christ, from whom the whole body, ... as each part is working properly, promotes the body's growth in building itself up in love' (Ephesians 4.15–16).

Every parish is unique, but the wind that blows through the church and the world blows through every parish. As society has become more diverse, so have individual churches. As groups in society have sought recognition and equality, so have groups within local churches. And as society has resisted the integration of those groups, so have local churches. The national church reflects and responds to the breezes and storms that blow through the churches, towns and cities of the nation; everything is connected.

The drama is played out, Sunday by Sunday. Newcomers arrive, bringing their hopes and their concerns, and are met by oldstagers. Those who have traditionally run and dominated the church see the wind of change beginning to blow, and respond according to their perception of the wind – whether it is seen as a hurricane, destroying all in its path, or as a cleansing breeze, removing the fog and smog of centuries.

St Peter's is no exception. If a social history of the life of the parish since 1970 was written, it would show that gradual, but fundamental and total change has taken place. The congregation in 1970 was entirely white and entirely working-class, as it had been for most of the 145 years of its previous existence. By 1980 there were a few Caribbean families sitting at the back but not seriously integrated into the life of the church. By 1990 there was a dawning recognition among the leadership of the need to involve the growing number of Africans and Caribbeans who, loyally and counterintuitively, continued to come to St Peter's. By 2000 the congregation had begun to include white professionals, black people made up around 70 per cent of the total attending, and the leadership reflected that – the first black churchwarden was appointed in 1999.

The really significant change in the life of the congregation – the 'Ephesians moment' – has taken place in the last three years. In the words of one Nigerian member of the congregation, 'St Peter's has become our church too. We remember who we are, now.' Tolerance has become welcome; acceptance has grown into inclusion. The dominant, historic culture of the church – high Anglican, white, led by the middle class and supported by the working class – has gradually been opened up to people of different ethnicities and different backgrounds.

Genuine efforts had been made previously to bring about stronger representation of the African congregation. But the expectation was that the culture would remain untouched; difference was welcome as long as it did not disrupt. African evenings were held, and well supported, on a Saturday night. Readers and intercessors were drawn from across the whole congregation. Many welcomed the greater breadth, although a few left, but it was skin-deep. Over the past three years, however, there have been many new developments in the life of the church. Two groups have begun – Wells, which reads relatively complex theological books and discusses them over a meal, and Rainbow, which offers 'entry level' discussion to new Christians. A gospel choir of twenty people from across the congregation has been started. Sunday School was renamed Junior Church and began to involve liturgy as well as teaching. Fresh Church, for 11–16-year-olds, takes place during the sermon and intercessions. A Mothers Union and a Men's Group have both started and very quickly found their place in the life of the church. Two services of affirmation of recent civil partnerships have taken place. A coffee morning aimed at young mothers with their children and the elderly (hoping for interaction between them) has begun, followed by a mid-morning mass. We have begun to offer 'Thanksgivings' during the service to celebrate happy events in people's lives. A Watch-Night service was introduced on New Year's Eve, which after only two years has become an inviolable tradition.

Each of these on their own is not especially significant. But taken together, they demonstrate that much is different throughout the church. The almost accidental combination of new things has had an effect beyond expectations. They have offered ways for people to celebrate their identity as part of particular groups, while at the same time remaining integral members of the church. The diversity of the congregation has been recognized and affirmed, without compromising the unity and community of the whole church. On the contrary; as people have become more recognized, the contacts and interaction between them have increased, so that the half-hour after church on Sundays has become much more lively, with more conversation and more friendship.

Part of this is to do with a slight growth in numbers attending, so that we have more resources to offer more activities, but a virtuous circle results – the more groups we have, the more engaged people become. None of it has been easy. Everyone is busy. Few have the time or energy for more church activities – understandably, given that many of the congregation work shifts or very long hours, or have young children (or both) or are retired and elderly with little energy to put into much beyond surviving. Besides, we have tried not to add to the already demanding tasks of holding down a job and/or bringing up children and/or maintaining a marriage or relationship. We have tried always to support and encourage people in their faith and in their lives and work, so that the church is subordinate to the people it tries to serve.

From tolerance to welcome; from acceptance to inclusion. From the margins to the mainstream. We have, to put it at its simplest, tried to make sure that each person has a place in the life of the church, not in spite of who they are but because of who they are – to offer a way of relating that is not either/or but both/and – both Nigerian and Anglican, both Christian and gay. Integration rather than dissolution. 'The eye cannot say to the hand, "I have no need of you", nor again the head to the feet, "I have no need of you"' (1 Corinthians 12.21). In Christ we have a new identity, but we do not leave our old identities behind. We meet, at the altar, with our human identities transformed and recognized by the love of Jesus Christ and in the power of the Spirit. Inclusion becomes exclusion when boundaries become barriers.

Exclusion takes place when the violence of expulsion, assimilation or subjugation and the indifference of abandonment replace the dynamics of taking in and giving out as well as the mutuality of giving and receiving ... What is exclusionary are the impenetrable barriers that prevent a creative encounter with the other.[5]

The experience of St Peter's and of many other churches is that challenging the sorts of exclusion that Paul rails against in the letter to the Galatians, but that are still very real today, need not be the cause of division. Splits and schisms are not necessary. Anglicanism has thrived for centuries recognizing diversity of worship and diversity of belief. Low church, broad church, high church. Urban, suburban, rural. Mass, Holy Communion, the Eucharist, the Lord's Supper. As the Bishop of Salisbury says, 'We are celebrating harmony, not peddling unison.'[6] How shall we sing the Lord's song in a strange land?

We are in a situation that is both modern and postmodern; both traditional and radically new. Our self-understanding as Christians and as human beings is both informed by the past and inspired by the present. We are members of small groups by which we define ourselves, we are inheritors of vast histories of state and nation by which we also define ourselves – and we are members together of the body of Christ.

---

5 Miroslav Volf, *Exclusion and Embrace*, 67.
6 David Stancliffe, July 2006, in a talk at Trafalgar, Salisbury.

5

'Shall I be leader?'

Toro Erogbogbo started coming to St Peter's when her son went to St Peter's School, in 1992. She came for a few years, but then started attending elsewhere because she did not feel that black people were included in the life of the church.

'I came to worship my God, because my son was at the school. But then it wasn't like it is now. It wasn't inclusive. Outside, in the churchyard, people wouldn't say hello. I thought, "I am here to serve my God and nobody can stop me coming here." But in the end I did stop coming, and went to another Anglican church because more of my people were there and they were welcomed.

'After you came I went to see you to ask for a confirmation certificate for my older son. You asked me if I would give out the wine at Communion. I said, "Your people will not take the wine from me." You said, "Let me sort that out." When I was approved to give out the wine I remember walking from my house to the church thanking God all the way.

'A few people left when black people started getting involved. But there were always new people coming in. When the old churchwardens retired, I asked you if it was possible. You said, "The position is available," and so I did it. I wanted my people to be included. I thought maybe Margaret (the other new churchwarden) wouldn't want to work with me – she was older, had been a priest's wife, was British, but she never looked down on me. We worked together all the time.

'When those families left the church I went to see them. "We cannot judge Giles," I said. "That is not for us. Think of what the church has done for you. You have brought your kids to church and sent them to secondary school. How can we judge him?"

'It was good, being churchwarden. My people were more included. Now we have two African churchwardens. It's always changing. We're always moving on.'

From before we are born until after our deaths, we are inextricably linked with institutions and institutional structures. The state provides ante-natal support, a new birth is registered, gas and water companies supply the means for hot water for washing. Schooling, safety, further education, law and order, government, clothing and food – everything depends on our engagement with structures far bigger than ourselves. Unless we seek to opt out entirely, creating an independent commune in the hills of Virginia, we cannot escape from them. But it is the tendency of institutions to seek to preserve themselves and to increase their power, often at the cost of others; and the tendency of people who have power within institutions to seek to preserve their own positions, often at the cost of others. The sight of presidents seeking to amend the constitutions of their own countries as their term of office comes to an end is all too frequent, as is the falsification of financial information in a company facing loss or bankruptcy.

The New Testament writers were much more familiar with the language of power and domination than the post-Enlightenment west. Angels and demons populate the world of the New Testament – 'To the angel of the church in Pergamum write: These are the words of him who has the sharp two-edged sword: I know where you are living, where Satan's throne is' (Revelation 2.12–13). The Gospel writers regularly speak of Jesus and the disciples' encounters with demons and demonic powers – 'That evening, at sundown, they brought to him all who were sick or possessed with demons ... and he cast out many demons; and he

would not permit the demons to speak, because they knew him'
(Mark 1.32–34).

The personification of institutions did not vanish with the Enlightenment, even if the language has changed. Companies are
seen as 'rock solid' or 'dodgy', as 'corrupt' or 'honest'; govern-
ments are admired as ethical or feared as despotic. Adam Smith
is credited with the creation of the notion of the 'invisible hand
of the market'. It is less well known that he was convinced it is
the role of business to serve the general welfare, and that profit
should be the reward that a business receives for such service.
The present triumph of market capitalism and the primacy of
profit – frequently involving the exploitation of people, the environment and the world's resources – is often interpreted as the
desertion by business of its fundamental responsibility to serve
its customers. Naomi Klein's writings, most famously *No Logo*,
are among the best-known exposures of the destructive potential of capitalism; her work is rebutted by those who see global
capitalism as a force for good.

The theologian Walter Wink, in his *Powers* trilogy – *Engaging the Powers*, *Unmasking the Powers* and *Naming the Powers*
– examines the relationship between what he terms 'The Powers
That Be' and God, humanity and the world.

Wink argues that

religious tradition has often treated the Powers as angelic or
demonic beings fluttering about in the sky. Behind the gross
literalism of that way of thinking, however, is the clear perception that spiritual forces impinge on and determine our lives.[1]

Institutions have a spiritual existence just as people have a spiritual existence.

The Powers are good
The Powers are fallen
The Powers must be redeemed.[2]

---

1 Walter Wink, *Engaging the Powers*, 3.
2 Walter Wink, *Engaging the Powers*, 3.

Religious institutions are as enmeshed as secular organizations in the temptations and distortions of what Wink calls the 'Domination Structures'. Despite the hope of the writer of the letter to the Ephesians

> This grace was given to me ... to make everyone see what is the plan of the mystery hidden for ages in God ... so that through the church [*ekklesia*] the wisdom of God in its rich variety might now be made known to the rulers and authorities in the heavenly places.
> Ephesians 3.8–10

the church still has far to go to make real the kingdom of God on earth. Compromised by state power, imbued with patriarchal values, often instruments of empire and domination, churches are as fallible as any other institution. But their fallibility is more apparent when set against their vocation – to live out and make manifest the unconditional love of God on earth.

The former president of Czechoslovakia, Václav Havel, observed that the line between resistance to and collaboration with the Communist regime ran through rather than round people. In the same way the line between good and evil runs through rather than round the churches. There are both angels and demons in the chancel. Wink's analysis of the influence and effect of the institutions around us is, itself, powerful, but it does not go far enough. All in positions of leadership and responsibility are themselves involved in the actions of organizations; they are both sinned against and sinning.

The relationship between the institution and the individual is symbiotic. A powerful institution confers power on those who are working for it. The employees are themselves given profit, power and status[3] as a result of the profit, power and status accrued by the organization. When the organization is threatened, the instinct of its members is to protect it. When the threat is serious, serious measures are taken in its defence. Equally, the

---

3 I am grateful to Ann Morisy for this categorization.

creative, life-enhancing and constructive aspects of an organization's life offer the potential for transformation to those who
are part of it. Inspiring leadership creates inspiration – destructive leadership brings destruction.

The philosopher Noam Chomsky has written extensively on
the way in which power obtains consent in democratic systems.
Writing especially about the United States, he identifies the way
in which a framework for 'acceptable' thought is established, so
that dissidence and opposition to the aims of the powerful are
reduced.

> It is necessary to establish a framework for possible thought
> that is constrained within the principles of the state religion.
> The critics reinforce this system by tacitly accepting these
> doctrines, and confining their critique to tactical questions
> that arise within them. To achieve respectability, to be ad-
> mitted to the debate, they must accept without question or
> inquiry the fundamental doctrine.[4]

Those who wish to participate in the dominant culture will
not rock the boat, so that they can be accepted; if they are too
subversive or disruptive they are cast out.

The other side of this process is that those who are part of
the system are encouraged into a sort of uniformity. There is no
overt censorship – particular kinds of behaviour, dress, opinion
are not specifically required. But people are expected to 'fit in',
not to misbehave or cause trouble. Newspaper proprietors with
strong political views do not have to check the articles in their
papers every day, for the editor knows what is expected and is
unlikely to risk her job by deliberately challenging the views of
the proprietor. Consent is assumed, and when consent is with-
drawn so is membership of the organization.

A church can function in the same way. The leadership does
not have to say what it wants, but if people wish to be involved
in the life of the church they know that there are ways in which

---

4 Chomsky, quoted in James Peck, *The Chomsky Reader*, 132.

they are expected to behave and opinions that are acceptable. They will not rock the boat as they fear losing their place in the community. Thus, a congregation can become formed in the image of the leadership. Especially in a typically western church context, where the leadership is usually white, male and middle-class, those who wish to be part of the church will consciously or unconsciously adopt behaviour that enables them to thrive within it. People from historically disempowered communities are unlikely to feel that the possibility is there to express their own cultural inheritance fully, to be themselves, to 'remember who we are'.

The Church of England remains overwhelmingly dominated by white, middle-class, mainly heterosexual men. Why? Partly the reasons are historic: the United Kingdom is, as well. But behind the obvious reasons are more subtle ones, and one of these is that the 'Androcentric White North Atlantic'[5] culture has been able to demand consensus by retaining its grip on the reins of power. So the church is not inclusive, because it does not celebrate diversity. Rather, it reshapes the other into what it wants her to be so that, in relation to her, it may be what it wants to be.

The leaders of churches, therefore, have an awesome respon-sibility. It is their task both to challenge the institution of which they are a part, and to build it. The church is as good, fallen and needing redemption as any bank, airline or media organization, and parishes and local churches are no less part of the dynamic of loss, discovery and reconciliation.

An inclusive church is a life-enhancing church. It is a church that celebrates creation rather than seeking to control it, ac-knowledging and welcoming the richness of God's love. A healthy church community will grasp the vision of the early church as described in the book of Acts, where all things were held in common and the people from all parts of the world understood the message in their own language, where the marks

---

5 Marcella Althaus-Reid, *From Feminist Theology to Indecent Theology*, 68.

of the Spirit – love, joy, generosity, self-control – were plain for all to see, and where there was a foretaste of the new heaven and the new earth. Inclusion does not define and is not defined by tradition or denomination, by churchmanship or particular interpretations of the Bible and history. Inclusive churches can be found across the theological and historical spectrum – evangelical, liberal and catholic, Nonconformist and Anglican, Catholic and Reformed. What they have in common is a self-understanding that is open to challenge, and a vision for the future that is confident and open. They are aware of their history but not bound by it – they are rooted in their past and looking to the future.

The photographic co-operative Magnum was formed after the Second World War by four news photographers – Robert Capa, Henri Cartier-Bresson, George Rodger and David 'Chin' Seymour. The aim was to offer photographers the chance to work independently, often without a commission, in the knowledge that their work could be sold or syndicated across the world. Cartier-Bresson described it as 'a community of thought, a shared human quality, a curiosity about what is going on in the world, a respect for what is going on and a desire to transcribe it visually'.[6] The co-operative is still thriving, 60 years later, because, according to Michael Ignatieff, 'The new generation [of photographers] seems to have understood the paradox that a great tradition forbids imitation and commands dissent from those who would wish to stay true to its essential vision.'[7]

There is a dynamic tension in church leadership that is unresolvable, because we are called to offer both continuity and change. We find ourselves in the roles of prophet, priest and pastor: prophet, calling the people into the wilderness, challenging them to tear down the structures that create oppression; priest, witnessing to the presence of God in the church and making God known among the people; and pastor, celebrating, grieving and walking alongside the people we are called to serve.

---

6 Henri Cartier-Bresson, interview with Hervé Guibert, *Le Monde*, 1947.

7 Michael Ignatieff, *Magnum*, 62.

The structures of exclusion are coterminous with the structures of injustice. It was the insight of the prophets of the Hebrew scriptures that God's love is the same as God's justice. 'What does the LORD require of you but to do justice, and to love kindness and to walk humbly with your God?' (Micah 6.8). One way in which the Powers exert their malevolent forces is by creating circumstances where the primary imperative is to preserve an identity and to keep others out, at all costs – at the cost of welcome, of integrity and of love. In apartheid South Africa, the Dutch Reformed Church (now at the forefront of the fight for racial justice) developed a theology that justified the exclusion of black people. The Church of England was not always in favour of the abolition of the slave trade – initially all the bishops of the Church of England voted against the abolition of slavery. Today there is continued exclusion of women from the episcopate and lesbian and gay people from full participation in the life of the church, and black and ethnic minority people are rarely able to take on positions of leadership. But the Powers work in more subtle ways, when children or the differently abled are not welcomed into the life of the church because of their potentially disruptive effects, or when an employer insists that staff work on a Sunday so that they cannot come to church, or when church bodies dispose of their rented housing to the highest bidder without regard for the communities involved, taking refuge in the law to justify their injustice.

If the heart of Christianity is the recognition that each of us is fully loved by God, each of us is separated from God and each of us can be redeemed by the saving love of Jesus Christ, then the Powers are manifesting their potential for evil every time a barrier is created that comes between us and God. Leadership is implicit in the potential for evil every time it supports exclusionary practices – every time it refuses recognition to a lesbian couple or to a woman offering herself as a leader, or fails to be sure that children can be part of worship too, or does not offer worship in which those who can scarcely read can be involved. A Christian leader, therefore, is called to seek out and challenge the ways in which her community is exclusionary, and to bring it to a place where the welcome offered is as close as possible to the welcome offered to each of us by God – and to seek out and challenge the ways in which she is part of that.

Fortunately, we have a model of Christian leadership that is without parallel and rich in lessons for pastors, priests and prophets. It is recounted in the four Gospels. As an example, the opening chapters of the Gospel of Mark describe how Jesus began his ministry and called his first disciples. John the Baptist arrives in the wilderness, proclaiming a new vision – the baptism of repentance and the forgiveness of sins. The people flock to him, clearly inspired. Jesus is baptized; and immediately develops the vision. 'The time is fulfilled, and the kingdom of God has come near; repent, and believe in the good news' (Mark 1.14). It may not have been quite clear to the people who, with alacrity, left everything and followed him; he may have been ahead on the 'vision thing'. But in spite of that, he built so much trust in his followers – his congregation – that they followed him at once, even though the promise they received was not a promise of a peaceful tranquil life but a promise of hard work – 'Follow me and I will make you fish for people' (Mark 1.17).

The next six chapters of the Gospel of Mark could be described as putting flesh on the dry bones of the vision of the kingdom of God. Through actions, teaching, debates and prayer, the dots are gradually joined and the picture becomes clearer. Jeffrey John's book, *The Meaning of the Miracles*, shows how each of the miracles that the writer of Mark describes is designed to manifest a breaking-down of exclusionary barriers and the bringing in of someone who was previously an outsider. The very first, the casting out of the unclean spirits (those demons again), makes that which was unclean, clean. Simon's mother-in-law, a woman, was healed and welcomed so that she could play her part again; and then throughout Galilee he 'cured many who were sick with various diseases, and cast out many demons' (Mark 1.34).

The challenges to the Pharisees about the status of the Torah, the parables and the miracles; all of these, taken together, are Jesus' way of showing the vision of the new heaven and the new earth and enabling those around him to understand and embrace it. But no sooner is Jesus named by Peter as the Christ, the Son of the Living God, than he begins to teach: 'If any want to become my followers, let them deny themselves, take up their cross and follow me' (Mark 8.34). Or, as the irritating catchphrase at St Peter's goes – 'Nobody said it was going to be easy.'

Then follows textbook good practice for organizational development. Constant in-service training as part of Jesus' succession planning enables the disciples to begin to take on leadership roles themselves. The establishing of a ritual meal creates a sense of corporate identity that will transcend geographical or ethnic boundaries, as well as ensuring the future well-being of those he intends to carry on his task. Only then is Jesus ready to follow the implication of the struggle for the reign of God to its ultimate conclusion and allow the Powers to imagine that they have won; and in the apparent victory comes their final defeat. This, says Henri Nouwen, a Catholic priest and writer on the spiritual life, is the ultimate model of leadership, the example that should be at the heart of Christian faith and practice:

I leave with you the image of a leader with outstretched hands, who chooses a life of downward mobility. It is the image of the praying leader, the vulnerable leader, and the trusting leader. May that image fill your hearts with hope, courage and confidence as you anticipate the next century.[8]

The story of the early church, as described in the Acts of the Apostles and the Epistles, can be read as the story of the first disciples struggling to apply the lessons they had learnt as they try to lead the new movement into the new Jerusalem. The battles with the Powers continue; Stephen is martyred for challenging the authorities. The battles with their own histories continue too; Peter has great difficulty recognizing the radically inclusive nature of the gospel, despite his dream at Joppa wherein all

8 Henri Nouwen, *In the Name of Jesus*, 96.

food was declared clean (Acts 10.9–17). The writings of Paul graphically illustrate the challenges of leadership; in the new world where Christ is the end of the law, how does a community of Christians thrive? 'You foolish Galatians ... The only thing I want to learn from you is this: Did you receive the Spirit by doing the works of the law or by believing what you heard?' (Galatians 3.1–2).

* * *

'I lift up my eyes to the hills – from where will my help come? My help comes from the LORD, who made heaven and earth.' (Psalm 121.1–2). St Peter's in 1998 was caught in a declining spiral. The front of the church has large wrought iron gates, designed by Sir John Soane. For much of the time they were closed. Its neoclassical façade has big black doors, which were also closed all day, every day, except on Sunday mornings. The paint was peeling from the doors; the noticeboards were cracked and faded, down to bare and rotting wood. The Sunday congregation had persuaded itself that the church was at risk of closure. The loyal and sacrificial efforts of a very few people – mainly the two churchwardens, the parish secretary and one non-stipendiary deacon – enabled the congregation to stumble on. In spite of that, the congregation was usually 50 or 60 on a Sunday – but at the end of my first Sunday service I went into the vestry to remove my chasuble and stole; when I came out of the vestry the church was almost empty.

It was the church's custom to advertise major services on a big board near the gates, at a cost of £30 per poster. There was insufficient money in the bank account to pay for posters, and so on the service sheet a couple of weeks before Ascension or Christmas there would be a note requesting a donation. Sometimes a donation was forthcoming; sometimes it wasn't. On the Monday morning after the first Sunday I went into the parish office and found, on my desk, a bill for central heating oil for £500. 'We should pay it', said the treasurer. 'Well let's, then', said I. 'We can't', he said. 'We only have £70 in the bank.'

The congregation was depressed. The angel of hope had been overcome by the demon of despair, and the church seemed to believe that repetition of its past was all that stood between it and oblivion. In such a situation the remedy is clear and simple to identify, although sometimes harder to put into effect. The first and most important thing, before any stewardship drives, any thoughts about repairing and renewing the building, any attempts to bring in new people or start new projects, is to begin to build a consensus of hope in the future.

The advantage in the situation at St Peter's was that the people were ready for a new vision; they positively wanted something that would take them out of the decline in which they felt themselves to be. So when, for my first sermon, I began to speak of a church that was, above all, 'Open, caring and prayerful', the response was immediate. Morning prayer at 8.30 the next morning was attended by five people; evening prayer by six. Tuesday the same, and Wednesday too. The briefest of conversations with the churchwardens brought me permission to open the gates and open the doors (there are glass doors inside the porch so that the building can remain secure) – although it was made clear that I would be to blame if vandals got in and desecrated the altar. Within two Sundays we had established that lay people could pray the Prayers of the People as well as reading the Bible, and two Sundays after that we'd also established that lay people, not in albs and not churchwardens, could give out Communion.

Each of these is a small step. But taken as a whole, they showed that the congregation was ready to embrace a new sense of itself; a sense that was characterized by optimism and confidence instead of despair and fear of failure. Back in 1998, 'inclusion' was not the buzz-word it is now. If it had been, the church would undoubtedly have said, 'We want to be an inclusive church'. And this was without, necessarily, knowing the full implications of that, but certainly believing that if it wanted to move into the future, the way was to be open, not closed.

How, then, is a Christian leader to find her way through the minefield with which she is presented? Perhaps the first requirement is to embrace the vision of the wholeness of humanity under God. The second is to have the ability to make mistakes and to recognize our own failures. The third is to embrace the tradition while at the same time enabling it to change, to embrace outsiders at the same time as offering insiders the comfort and continuity they need. And the fourth is to have the courage to take risks, in the knowledge that sometimes things will go wrong.

'Thus says the Lord GOD: I will soon lift up my hand to the nations, and raise my signal to the peoples; and they shall bring your sons in their bosom, and your daughters shall be carried on their shoulders' (Isaiah 49.22). The task of a leader of a Christian community is not simply to accept but positively to welcome the complexities of human diversity. The joy visible in a community that has embraced the distinctiveness of all its members is a joy that results from recognizing that Mary, 67, with significant mental health problems but with a succinct wisdom appreciated by all, is chatting to Remi, 36, senior barrister for the Crown Prosecution Service; that Charlie and Jeremy's service of thanksgiving for their civil partnership was attended by Naomi, 72, from Sierra Leone, who had been brought up to think that gay people deserved death. The tone for this kind of welcome comes from the breadth of acceptance in the leadership team. Welcome involves trust; Mary is invited to set up the Lady Chapel for teenagers' church and Naomi is responsible for organizing the coffee morning on Thursdays. As those on the edge are brought into the centre, the centre becomes wider. The network of relationships becomes more complex. People take more pride in their community, and from that begin to take on more responsibility. Sometimes it doesn't quite work. Edges are rough, and some people are keen to take control. The community of God's reign does not run as smoothly as the well-oiled machinery of a West End show. Its depth and its life come from the tiny interactions of a team at work – which are often to do with managing failure rather than celebrating perfection.

The leadership team too is helped if it has the grace to acknowledge its own imperfections. To say sorry for lateness, or acting thoughtlessly, or not thinking something through, or having expectations of someone that are not realized. To see and act upon the moments when trust was misplaced – not withdrawing trust but changing the requirements, perhaps. Accepting the need for training, so that each can become confident in the other and the place becomes a 'learning organization' moving forward, rather than a complacent organization resting in a backwater. But the leadership team, be it lay or ordained, also has the privilege and opportunity to lead others into transformation, to hold them as they seek their own vulnerabilities, to support them in their journeys and to inspire them to take risks that lead them into new places.

One fundamental way of doing this is through prayer – through ensuring that people of the church are supported and encouraged in their lives of prayer and through trying to make sure that the church itself is a place of prayer and lively spirituality. The discipline of daily prayer, perhaps in the morning and the evening, is a wonderful gift. At its best, and if carried out in a public place of worship, it can bring together a praying community steeped in the Psalms and the scriptures and be a firm foundation and a place of support and inspiration for the life and work of the church.

To embrace the tradition while enabling it to change is hard. Change management is taught little at seminaries. Trust and vision are essential commodities. The community (not every single member but a majority) needs to trust the people implementing change – to be able to be sure that their commitment is to the 'soul' of the church. The community, also, needs to be heard. Consultation and listening are paramount. For me, the church council's ability to work out a new vision was unlocked when I read Nancy Kline's book on management technique *Time to Think: Listening to Ignite the Human Mind*. The very simple technique of going round a meeting, inviting each person in turn to speak for up to three minutes without fear of interruption, often leads to a remarkable consensus as well as enabling the more shy or unconfident people to be heard. Often the quietest people are the wisest. Outsiders and insiders, newcomers and old lags have their say.

{76}

Once a vision is established – 'Ho, everyone who thirsts, come to the waters; and you that have no money, come, buy and eat!' (Isaiah 55.1) – the tradition can be adapted to serve it. Resistance to drinking coffee in the body of the church instead of in the hall has disappeared as people have recognized that the whole community benefits from the presence side by side of those who do not drink coffee and those who do – a small but significant change.

But sometimes it is necessary to push the envelope further than the community is willing to entertain. It is necessary to go out on a limb, to act in spite of resistance, whether that resistance arises from fear, an opposition group or deeply held sentiment. Risk is a vital part of the life we are called to lead. Edward Patey writes, 'If anyone needs to be persuaded that God is a risk-taker, he has only to look at the people he calls to be his agents. Many priests and faithful laity discover an exhilaration as they come to know themselves as part of God's risk-taking enterprise.'[9]

One final point on leadership. The church is not unique in having a high proportion of middle-class people on its management teams, but it probably has a higher than average level of 'middle-class cringe' – the belief that the actions and opinions of the well off and well educated are less valid than those of the poor and the marginal. The South African Albie Sachs was a prominent member of the fight against apartheid in the 1960s and 1970s. When a bomb exploded in his car in 1988, he lost an arm, and the sight in one eye, and suffered hearing loss and the loss of the use of his legs. His story of the struggle back to health after the bomb blast, *The Soft Vengeance of a Freedom Fighter*, includes extended reflections on the complexities of being a Jewish white male involved in the fight for freedom for black and coloured people. He relates an encounter with a flower seller that ends:

I am sorry I did not buy even more flowers, and feel more convinced than ever that those of us born into privilege should

9 Edward Patey, *Faith in a Risk-Taking God*, 127.

not waste time on despising ourselves, but get on as robustly and effectively as possible with the job of pouring into the struggle everything we have been fortunate to acquire, our knowledge, our vision, our culture, while we enrich our lives with the one thing our privilege denied us, sensitivity to the culture and longings of the oppressed.[10]

10 Albie Sachs, *The Soft Vengeance of a Freedom Fighter*, 192.

6

Limitless Freedom?

*Alan Wild was a 'reluctant Christian'. He drifted into St
Peter's in 1978, a couple of months after his wife, Eileen,
started attending on Sundays – which was the result of their
son going to the local church school.*

'I caught the vision. The message said something to me.
My first Good Friday it hit home – that someone was prepared to sacrifice himself just for me. The hopelessness of
Good Friday followed by the hope, the gladness and the love
of Easter Day – gave me the knowledge that there's more to
this life, something after that's better.*

'Paul [Jobson, Rector at the time] latched on to order and
presentation, so I did too. It fitted with my job as a printer.
Balance, how things look – it matters. I became a server and
made sure everything was as near perfect as I could get it.'

*After becoming a server, Alan began to be encouraged to
think about ordination. He was ordained priest in the Local
Ordained Ministry stream the same month I arrived as
Rector.*

'Inclusion hadn't really been an issue until then, although
Gordon [Murray, my predecessor] had brought new people
in, especially some black people. Then everything changed.
Getting more people to do the jobs. It was hard for me at
first, handing over. I used to do things for the people I was
supposed to be handing over to, not telling them. But then
I thought, you have to let people be who they are. I had to
accept that things might not be as sharp and as square as*

I liked them, but that's them. That's the real challenge. But we're pretty good at it now, I think, a lot better than we were. I learnt that you can surrender that comfort zone without compromising too much. And you can see people enjoying it. It's better. There are more surprises, and if you just have the same people doing the same things you can become stale. And if you're open you can tap into all those different experiences.

'No, inclusion's not "anything goes". There's a divine spark inside everyone and if you're serving them you're serving God. That's the text that we follow, the example of our Lord himself – it didn't matter who they were or what they are, the church is full of sinners or there wouldn't be a church! By inviting people we know who they are and we hear their story. Even if it's a notorious drug user or murderer you'd sometimes get a glimpse of God's love shining through that darkness.

'It's not a free for all, though. If it became too rough and ready it wouldn't be what it is. The sacrament is between them and their God but we have to make sure it's adminis-tered properly. That's service too.

'When you came, and told me you were gay, I had to think about it. For the first time, really. I came to the conclusion, "What's all the fuss about? At the end of the day, it's purely and simply about love. How dare we say someone shouldn't be included? I look at Jason and don't say, that's Jason who's gay. I say, that's Jason."'

The sheer, luxurious extravagance of grace. The boundless ocean of the love of God. The awe and mystery of the infinity of God, haltingly described by the Psalmist or grasped at in the extraordinary visions of Ezekiel and the Revelation of John. The incommensurable, untouchable and unrestrained torrent of love that flows from God into the world. A symphony written for eternity and played by the galaxies and stars; an eruption of wonder into creation and the transformation of nothingness into everything.

A half-empty church on Sunday morning, with a few loyal souls shuffling up to the altar rail to receive a dry wafer of unleavened bread and a sip of sweet wine, after muttering a couple of hymns and grunting a few quiet amens. A tired minister takes off her robes in the vestry and potters home along rainy streets, half acknowledging the half acknowledgements from passersby. A lonely man joins the lunch group for their weekly trip to Ribs Delicious and together they touch briefly on the sermon before turning to more exciting matters – *Strictly Come Dancing*, perhaps, or another political scandal.

The scriptures and the great religious writers and mystics are searching for words to describe the indescribable sense of the love of God. Saint Teresa of Avila, Mother Julian of Norwich, John of the Cross, the Desert Fathers, the writers of Revelation or Ezekiel or the Gospels – are all trying to communicate, to tell the world of the encounter they have had with that which is utterly beyond words – the peace of God that passes all understanding.

Jesus, too, in his parables, continually emphasizes the extravagant and counterintuitive grace of God in which the world is drenched. There are many examples in the parables – of the vineyard, with the labourers receiving the same whether they had worked for ten hours or one, or of the seed that falls on good soil, springing up and yielding thirty-, sixty- or one hundredfold, or of the wedding banquet when, we are told, the host said to his servants – 'Go out into the roads and lanes, and compel people to come in, so that my house may be filled' (Luke 14.23). The miracles too are stories of the unquenchable love of God – the changing of water into 40 gallons of wine, the feeding of 5,000 people with enough left over to fill 12 baskets. 'Happy are the people who know the festal shout, who walk, O Lord, in the light of your countenance; they exult in your name all day long, and extol your righteousness' (Psalm 89.15–16).

There are two common criticisms of inclusive theology. First, that it means that anything goes – that any kind of behaviour is acceptable in the house of God, that there are no limits to what a person may or may not do and still be welcome or that notorious sinners can roll up to church and, without so much as a nod towards repentance or transformation, can be included in the life of the church. Second, that inclusion is itself deeply exclusive – it does not welcome those who disagree with it, those who, for example, reject the ordination of women or the presence of gay clergy with partners as parish priests.

Paul, formerly Saul, Rabbi and Jew, was presented with a conundrum once he had accepted that Christ is the Messiah. In the earliest years of Christianity, followers of Christ had not separated themselves from the rest of Judaism – relationships with the synagogues and temple continued until the fall of Jerusalem in 70 CE. But Judaism was by its nature an exclusive religion, dependent on birth and inheritance, and in spite of the universal vision of some of the prophets there were very definitely limits to inclusion in first-century Israel. One of the principal charges against Jesus was that he broke the limits and went outside the boundaries of acceptable behaviour for a Jew.

The People of God founded their identity in the blood line they believed they shared, descending from Adam via Abraham, and in the shared code of behaviour set out in the Torah. To be one of the Chosen People was to be a descendant of Abraham with the responsibility of observing the law and honouring the prophets; to have a particular relationship with the land of Israel and Judah, and to honour Yahweh, God, as the only God. To be one of the Chosen People was to be inside the circle; to be Gentile was to be outside.

The third chapter of Galatians confronts head-on the question of how the promise made to Abraham, and believed by the Jews to apply only to his descendants, can be understood if at the heart of Paul's new faith is salvation of all peoples. Paul was not about to throw out his heritage, and yet at the same time he knew that the message he had was a universal message, for all people.

Miroslav Volf, extrapolating from N. T. Wright's *The Climax of the Covenant*, identifies three steps that Paul takes in order to move from the particular to the universal. First, he relativizes the Torah. If the Torah cannot produce the universal human family implied by faith in one God and Jesus Christ his son, it cannot be God's final word. Second, 'for the sake of equality Paul discards genealogy'[1] – the promise 'had to be by faith, so that it could be according to grace: otherwise there would be some who would inherit not by grace but as of right, by race'.[2] And third, Paul identifies Christ as the offspring of Abraham in whom the promise is to be fulfilled: 'Now the promises were made to Abraham and to his offspring; it does not say, "And to offsprings" as of many; but it says "And to your offspring", that is, to one person, who is Christ' (Galatians 3.16). So Christ is the descendant of Abraham, and faith in Christ makes us each a descendant of Abraham and therefore an inheritor of the promise.

God is one. God is universal. At the end of Galatians 3, we reach the resounding statement cited in Chapter 3 above, – 'the magna carta of Pauline egalitarianism and universalism'[3] – 'There is no longer Jew or Greek, there is no longer slave or free, there is no longer male and female; for all of you are one in Christ Jesus. And if you belong to Christ, then you are Abraham's offspring, heirs according to the promise' (Galatians 3.28–29). For Paul, there are no limits to the love of God. The whole world is called to become one in Christ Jesus.

End of subject, one might hope. In theory, yes: for the churches should place no limit on baptism, and the sacrament of the Eucharist is available to all the baptized (in some churches, after confirmation; in others, from the moment of baptism). But in reality this is not the case. Generations of Christians beyond Paul have placed the strictest of limits on the availability of the sacraments and the inclusivity of the Christian gospel. The superabundance of the heavenly banquet has been replaced by the pinched resistance of churches distressingly keen to shut out rather than to bring in; the radical welcome of Jesus' message

---

1 Miroslav Volf, *Exclusion and Embrace*, 45.
2 N. T. Wright, *The Climax of the Covenant*, 168.
3 Miroslav Volf, *Exclusion and Embrace*, 45.

has been replaced by an image of God limited by the boundaries of our fear.

Paul embraces universalism so that all can be welcomed by God to the eucharistic table. In the New Testament, that universalism never becomes a force for the imposition of a coercive sameness. The differences between communities and people are not denied or ignored, and the unity of peoples before God is not collapsed into uniformity. At Pentecost, we are told, the disciples did not speak one language, they spoke many – the languages of the Parthians, the Medes, the Elamites, the residents of Mesopotamia, Judea and Cappadocia, Pontus and Asia ... Pentecost was no return to the pre-Babel days when all spoke the same tongue – on the contrary, each language became a means of communication for the grace of God. Difference is celebrated within the history of early Christianity – we hear, in the New Testament, of the Galatians, the Romans, the church at Pamphylia, the church in Corinth, each with their particular issues and problems and their particular virtues and solutions.

But since then, and with the rise of institutional churches, the powerful have set the criteria for membership, and those who are not part of the majority – the disabled, the elderly, gay people, women – have been silenced or marginalized. The emphasis on 'the family' and on marriage is a manifestation of this; single people have spoken of their sense of being on the margins of some churches where the overwhelming majority are young, married and with children.

The message given by Jesus over and over again is that it is not only the rich and the successful, the holy and the righteous, who are invited to the banquet of the kingdom; it is the poor, the outcast, those who are damaged and broken, those who make their money by illegal and illegitimate means, the *'anawim'*. Widows and orphans, sinners and prostitutes, tax collectors, transsexuals, Romans and Pharisees. All are called into relationship with God, and all are invited to the table. That God's grace is available to all, indiscriminately, is symbolized by the way in which the Church of England and most other churches are willing to baptize infants, long before they have the power of decision or even the power to speak. Babies are baptized in the hope that they will be brought up to an understanding of the Christian faith, but much more in the confidence that God's grace will rest upon them. The history of missionary activity is chequered, but behind it lies the belief that the grace of God should be available to all, expressed in the sacrament of baptism.

At the eucharistic table God is calling each person into relationship with Godself. That relationship will, by definition, require believers to make changes, to amend their behaviour; to turn away from sin and be faithful to Christ. We are presented with an invitation into the fullness of love, which speaks into our situation of brokenness and pain. To become whole we are invited to leave our brokenness behind; to move from behaviour and situations that are harmful and destructive to those that are creative and fulfilling. Our relationship with God calls us deeper and deeper into relationship with that which is good, and the process of repentance, which means, literally, turning back, is the process of leaving the harmful behind and turning to the good.

Each person starts from a place that is both broken and redeemed. We are all involved in forms of behaviour that are individually or institutionally destructive. For the wealthy and powerful the danger can be economic exploitation of others, or a failure to acknowledge their own vulnerability and need of love. For the poor, it is often a sense of their own inadequacy and hopelessness in the face of a world that appears uncaring. The obvious sins, of dependency on sex or drugs or power, compete with the less obvious sins of complacency or selfishness. Idolatry takes many forms, from the most obvious – love of money – to the most dangerous – exaltation of a constituent part of religion (the church, the Bible) over and above the God at the heart of faith.

It is the role of the church to be a means of grace and to enable the world to receive the sacraments, not to limit access to them. We are all guests at the table of the Lord; some of us pour the wine or break the bread, but all of us are guests. We are all invited. But although the invitation is there, it is not always accepted. Or it is accepted half-heartedly; the wedding garment is not worn and the guest is 'thrown into the outer darkness, where there will be weeping and gnashing of teeth' (Matthew 22.13). If we are called to repentance but choose not to abandon the behaviour that is standing between us and fullness of life, we are not wholeheartedly accepting the invitation to the banquet; we are standing outside the door looking in; we are excluding ourselves. But that must be our decision, not the church's.

The Gospels tell, again and again, of Jesus' ability to go to the heart of what is destructive in a person. In Luke, for instance, when the ruler comes to ask Jesus what he must do to inherit eternal life, 'Jesus looked at him and said, "How hard it is for those who have wealth to enter the kingdom of God!"' (Luke 18.24). Not all those who came to Jesus and were wealthy were told to sell everything; Zacchaeus, the tax collector, for example, only had to give away half of his wealth as well as making restitution to those he had defrauded. Repentance requires different actions from different people. It is preceded by an awareness of God's welcome. The woman at the well, to whom Jesus speaks at length despite the fact that she was clearly ostracized and an outcast, rushes back to the town saying, 'Come and see a man who told me everything I have ever done!'; for her, the simple and welcoming way in which Jesus speaks to her is enough to make her question, 'He cannot be the Messiah, can he?' (John 4.29).

Paul's concern was to ensure that in place of the law did not come anarchy but love. The notorious passages in the Epistles (among those texts often referred to as 'Texts of Terror'[4]) that forbid women to speak in church, that are thought to condemn same-sex relationships, that appear to condone slavery and the place of men at the head of the hierarchy, were written to particular churches in particular situations. He nurtured and cared for new communities that were learning for the first time what it meant to believe that the one who was awaited had come, and that the world is truly drenched in grace. His furious denun-

---

4 The phrase was originally used by Phyllis Trible.

ciation of the inappropriate relationship in 1 Corinthians; his pulling up of the people of Corinth for their disrespect of the Eucharist where the rich ate plenty and the poor had nothing; his recommendations about the behaviour of women in church and of men in the home; these were all part of his desire to ensure that the fledgling communities functioned properly, as images of the new reign of God that has come about through the crucifixion and resurrection of Christ.

Being inclusive does not and can never mean condoning or accepting destructive relationships and behaviours. Paedophilia, for example, is always and everywhere wrong because it involves, by definition, abuse. Other forms of exploitative or loveless sexuality, other breaches of contract (adultery) and other forms of behaviour that oppress or destroy – dishonesty, environmental destruction, financial exploitation, murder – have no part in an inclusive theology or in an inclusive church. Inclusion and sin are incompatible. If the will of God is for each person to live life in the fullest abundance imaginable, then the limits of inclusion are set at the point where relationship tips into oppression or lovelessness – or where behaviour becomes destructive of self, of others or of faith. A theology of inclusion must be clear about this, but it must also be clear that the sacrament, the love of Jesus, can, if it is allowed to, bring about change in even the most seemingly hopeless and desperate situations. Repentance transforms, and in breaking down the barriers to inclusion the hope is that the love of God will become apparent even to those who imagine themselves to be well outside its reach.

An inclusive church will not condone destructive behaviour. But neither will it exclude people from access to God's grace. As quoted at the beginning of the chapter, Alan Wild says:

Even if it's a notorious drug user or murderer you'd sometimes get a glimpse of God's love shining through that darkness. It's not a free for all, though. If it became too rough and ready it wouldn't be what it is. The sacrament is between them and their God but we have to make sure it's administered properly. That's service too.

That begs the question whether it is sometimes necessary for people to set limits to their own freedom, in the interests of the whole community or of those around them. Paul addresses this in the controversy over the consumption of food sacrificed to idols: 'But take care that this liberty of yours does not somehow become a stumbling-block to the weak' (1 Corinthians 8.9). Of course, love calls us to act with respect for our fellow human beings. The example of eating food sacrificed to idols, against which Paul advises because it may confuse those with less knowledge, is apposite. In the same way we are called to be careful in the way in which we preach or teach or do our theology because there are always some in a parish for whom faith is a simple thing with certainties and imperatives that, when challenged, can bring fear, insecurity or anger. But restraint should not be an excuse for stasis – it is often those in power who appeal for restraint for the sake of 'the weak' and those on the outside who are asked to moderate their calls for inclusion for the sake of not upsetting the apple cart. The furore that greeted the former Bishop of Durham, David Jenkins, after his perfectly reasonable questions about the nature of faith and the meaning of the resurrection, is an example of the way in which proper theological endeavour and thought is often stifled by people resisting change.

If God is inviting each of us to the fullness of our personhood as individuals and members of the church – then we should be extremely cautious about asking, say, for the consecration of women as bishops to be delayed for the sake of those who in conscience can't accept their ministry. Revd Lee Tim-Oi, the first woman to be ordained as priest in the Anglican Communion, with great grace refrained from acting out her priesthood until the Communion as a whole had agreed that such a development was possible. There are certainly times when it is right and proper to hold back from actions for the sake of the whole church. But when the argument that calls for protection of the weaker brethren is used to resist the full inclusion of members of the body of Christ – particularly when it is used by those who have traditionally held power in the church – it should be viewed with profound suspicion. Too often, the 'good of the church' has been cited as a means of maintaining exclusion. As members of the church we have a responsibility for one another, but that applies to all – not only those who seek change but also those who resist it. The needs of the weaker brethren should not be used as an excuse for inaction or resistance to God's call.

What, then, of those who hold views and positions that are fundamentally at odds with an inclusive theology? Those who would not support the priesthood or episcopate of women or who are unwilling to recognize the holiness of same-sex relationships? Does an inclusive theology exclude them?

The Anglican Communion is struggling to avoid a schism that is threatened because agreement cannot be reached about the welcome it can offer to lesbian, gay, bisexual and transgendered (LGBT) Christians. In this context, the crucial question is whether people who fundamentally disagree are able together to be part of a church that has traditionally tried to keep its doors open wide so that all may come in. One of the most disgraceful episodes in the Anglican Communion in the last ten years was at Dromantine in Northern Ireland, where the Primates of the Provinces of the Communion were gathered in February 2005. Over ten primates absented themselves from a Eucharist celebrated by the Archbishop of Canterbury because of the presence of the Presiding Bishop of the Episcopal Church of the United States, who had supported the consecration of Gene Robinson as Bishop of New Hampshire.

If an inclusive theology is truly lived out, it will make no distinctions on the basis of gender, sexuality or ethnicity. But there are those in the church who are unwilling or unable to acknowledge the grace of God working in and through the priesthood or episcopate of women or through the ministry of those in same-sex relationships – who, because of their interpretation of the gospel, see these things as inimical to Christianity. They will find themselves ill at ease or unable to be part of an inclusive community because of the values it holds. But the crucial point is that they are, in their unwillingness to comprehend God's grace in the world, excluding themselves. Just as some left St

Peter's when Africans became more involved in the service, so some are unable to remain in a church that welcomes women and LGBT people fully and equally. The conflicts within the Anglican Communion are a working-out globally of the dynamic tension between inclusion and exclusion. In the end, it is not possible to accommodate both. But it is not inclusive theology that excludes; it is the inability to recognize the Holy Spirit at work in the world.

We are guardians of the faith as it has been received by us. The churches have a responsibility to hand on that faith to generations yet unborn and to those who have not yet received it. Just as the sacraments are the outward and visible sign of inward invisible grace, so the life and work of the church must, as far as possible, be a sign of the universal grace of the love of God. The economy of grace has primacy over the economy of moral deserts. As Jürgen Moltmann says in *The Crucified God*, 'fearful faith arises wherever the gospel of creative love for the abandoned is replaced by the law of what is supposed to be Christian morality, and by the penal law'.[5]

It is God who invites us to come, and it is for the church to communicate the invitation. But simply to say that all are welcome is rarely enough. 'We tried that, and no one came.' How are we to live out our calling, making sure that everyone who may be on the margins of the church – whether because they are too young or too old, too noisy, too disabled, women, gay or black – is brought into the centre? How are we to make sure that no one is outside the circle?

---

5 Jürgen Moltmann, *The Crucified God*, 14.

7

From the Margins to the Centre

Margaret and Elisha Temenu were born and brought up in Lagos. They attended St Peter's Anglican Church in Lagos, and so when they moved to Walworth in the 1970s it was natural for them to start coming to St Peter's. They are committed Anglicans for whom missing church on a Sunday is not an option. They attended loyally for about ten years, but during that time no real effort was made to include them. Along with others, they found that members of the church were – with some shining exceptions – rarely friendly in the street, and the responsibilities and jobs were much more frequently shared among those people who had been in the church for a long time. After staying for as long as they could bear it, they left St Peter's and tried a local church. But its style of worship did not sit comfortably with their tradition, and so they began to go to Southwark Cathedral.

'But now it's all quite different. We came back to our church. It's so different. Everyone is included. Everyone is welcome. Now people talk to us in the street. When I was in hospital people came to visit me. We care for each other now and the black people are there in the centre of the church with everybody else. In the services we have African things sometimes.'

During 2005 a documentary was screened on Channel 4 called Gay Vicars. *I was interviewed for the programme. Nobody commented much on it afterwards, except to say that they'd seen it, but two families stopped coming. I was sad about that, particularly as they hadn't spoken to me about it and did not return my calls. But a year later I discovered that, after these families had left, Margaret and Toro (who was then churchwarden) had, without telling me, gone round to see the families who had left, not to support them in their decision but to say that they were being sinful for not supporting me their priest as I had been supporting them for many years.*

After the Watch Night service in 2006 Margaret said, 'First we found we could have our church back. And now we can remember who we are.'

From my first year at St Peter's I was regularly asked by West African members of the congregation if we were to have a Watch Night service that year. What's Watch Night? I asked. It's New Year's Eve, I was told, and it is our custom to go to church for midnight. I quickly took the decision that St Peter's would not have a Watch Night service as it would create a precedent and become a tradition from which we would have trouble moving away should future ministers wish to have New Year's Eve to themselves.

After eight years, with a team of four clergy, and having been asked each year if we were to have a Watch Night service and having repeated my previous answer, we decided that the time had come to attempt such a service. Advertising it quietly and unobtrusively, we prepared a short liturgy of thanksgiving, with a couple of hymns, and opened the doors at 11.00.

By 11.30 there were 100 people there, and as midnight approached the church became more and more full. Quickly more service sheets were copied, and our anticipation of a short, quiet service was transformed. We had no organist, having been unable to find one, with the result that the singing was chaotic; and the service itself was not exactly a liturgical triumph.

But that didn't matter. What mattered was that we had finally, after years of denial, recognized the need to offer a service to the West African congregation that reflected their tradition and enabled them to participate in Christian spirituality in a way that was in many ways more significant than Midnight Mass is for the white British population of Walworth.

The reaction of the African members of the congregation was very clear. They were delighted that we had, after so long, finally recognized the importance to their spirituality and their tradition of a Watch Night service. Even though it wasn't exactly what they were used to and didn't quite work, liturgically, nonetheless it was a powerful acknowledgement of their culture and history.

After the service we set about researching what should have happened, and discovered after much questioning that it should have begun at 11 o'clock with hymns and prayers, with long intercessions for family, church and world, and moved into the prayer of consecration shortly after midnight so that the Eucharist could be celebrated in the New Year. We held a Watch Night mass on 31 December 2007 attended by 200 people, as did other churches in the deanery; the tradition is now established.

Inclusive Church held its first residential conference in November 2007, entitled 'Drenched in Grace'. The overwhelming response to the conference was that it was a great success; we were graced with excellent presentations by our speakers, and the spirit and the atmosphere of the conference were unique in many participants' experience. Young and old, straight and gay, transsexual, black, white, single and married all pursuing with passion the vision of a Christianity truly welcoming against a background of an apparently disintegrating Anglican Communion.

There were two undercurrents of concern – first, to do with the language of the liturgy, which was insufficiently inclusive for some, referring to the first person of the Trinity as Father and using the masculine pronoun, and second, to do with a perception of 'gayness' within the conference. Much reflection on this led me to ask whether the questions that arose manifested something I had not previously taken on board, which is that people have very different expectations and understandings of inclusion and of being an inclusive church, and that a truly inclusive church is presented with significant challenges if it is both to acknowledge and to celebrate the differences between us.

For most women, sexuality expressed by men towards them has been oppressive; their bodies have been objectified and their personhood diminished by a power relationship that has throughout history been one of subjugation and marginalization. So oblique sexual references are seen as a manifestation of historical oppression. For gay men, though, the suppression of sexuality has been the main means of their oppression by those with power; gay men have been forced to deny and hide their sexuality with the result that their personhood has been diminished by repression. In that context, the expression of sexuality can be seen as liberating rather than oppressive, as a source of expression rather than repression. So we have diametrically different understandings of language, both valid, and both rooted in the experience of marginalization and exclusion.

Across the country, church doors are opened every Sunday morning, and during the week. We hope that people will come in; we circulate leaflets in the parish and put notices up outside; we highlight special services on our websites and tentatively try new things, 'Fresh Expressions', in the hope that they will attract fresh congregations. At times, we look at the congregation and we are pleased by the way in which it seems to contain people from many places and many backgrounds. But, at the same time, there may be a nagging doubt, a question in the back of our minds. Somehow, it seems as though it's not quite right. The enthusiasm hoped for isn't there. The people are there in body but the spirit seems to be absent. Loyal and dutiful attendance is not translating into profound commitment, and sometimes it seems as though the stone rolled up the hill over and over again is in danger of becoming stuck at the bottom. There may be a thousand presenting reasons why the hopes are not fulfilled. But underneath it, there may be something fundamental happening that is acting as a barrier to new life, as a brick wall that stops progress and does not allow the church community to live out the fullness of its life.

The questions over the Watch Night service at St Peter's and over Drenched in Grace highlighted, for me, something I had failed to recognize previously, in my work and ministry. I had failed to recognize and to hear the needs and the dreams of the communities I was trying to serve. Although, alongside the other members of the leadership team, I had tried to offer what I thought was appropriate, and supported the communities in ways that seemed right, beneath it I had not tried to understand what fundamentally made them tick – what motivated them and inspired them and challenged them and made them cry. It was enough that they came to church; because they were in church I assumed that they were being nourished, fed and supported. But shortly after Louise arrived as curate at St Peter's in 2006, she said, 'I want to make sure the Africans are included.' I was surprised at that – I thought they were already.

People from ethnic minorities and black people have been, and remain, excluded from many mainstream churches. Not in numbers – particularly not in the inner cities, where they easily make up the majority of church members and ensure that churches that would have long since closed remain open – but in terms of authority, influence, power and respect, black people are at the margins of the structures. The fact that the Church of England has a black Archbishop of York and a Bishop of Rochester of Asian extraction does little to alter the fundamental perception that it is difficult for black people to become fully part of the church. Minority ethnic representation on our local diocesan synod and on the General Synod of the Church of England actually decreased in the 2006 elections.

I try not to talk about different ethnic and cultural groups in terms of 'race'. The notion of different races, being defined by physical characteristics, such as (predominantly) skin colour, hair type and facial characteristics emerged during the late eighteenth and early nineteenth centuries as European scientists began to classify humanity in the same way that it sought to classify the natural world. 'Race' is a concept that goes hand in hand with empire: 'the theorists, all North Europeans, were agreed on, unsurprisingly, the superiority of North Europeans in intelligence and morality'.[1] The findings of genetics have demonstrated that there are tiny differences between the genomes of people of different ethnicities, and sociological studies have demolished the notion that there are inherent character differences. 'We recommend avoiding using the word "race" to refer to particular groups of people instead of humanity as a whole.'[2]

'Yes,' said a friend, 'there is no such thing as race, only racism.' Whether overt or covert, whether institutional or personal, people are still discriminated against on the basis of their colour and origin, both within and outside the church. The church has many times expressed its desire to ensure that black people play a full part in its life; why, then, is it not happening? Why are Pentecostal and black-led churches flourishing while mainstream churches are struggling, even in the inner cities? And why are we not able, yet, to celebrate the richness of humanity within our churches?

History has a great deal to do with it. The Bible has been used as to justify oppression of black people by white people – not just in apartheid South Africa by the Dutch Reformed Church but also in the United States and the UK.

Eighteenth-century white Christians turned to the Bible and read Genesis 9.18–27, the 'Curse of Ham,' as God's punishment for black sin and intention for the races: 'Cursed be Canaan; the lowest of slaves shall be he to his brothers.' In this theological construction of race, God placed those of European descent as a master class over a slave class of Africans, 'and let Canaan be his slave.'[3]

The dominant culture of the mainstream churches is one that does not reflect the dominant cultures of black and minority ethnic people; result, exclusion. Doreen's mum being turned away; services being white-dominated and white-led. Culture – in Charles Handy's definition, 'the way we do things here'

---

1 Linbert Spencer, *Building a Multi-ethnic Church*, 16.
2 Linbert Spencer, *Building a Multi-ethnic Church*, 17.
3 Horace Griffin, *Their Own Receive Them Not*, 23.

– has an insidious power that undermines, often fatally, the best of intentions to include, be open and make welcome.

As in so much else, the New Covenant turns this upside-down – developing the radical inclusion called for by some of the prophets and the imperative within the Hebrew Scriptures to care for the widow, the orphan and the alien. 'He has sent me ... to let the oppressed go free, to proclaim the year of the Lord's favour' (Luke 4.18). In more subtle ways we see the radically inclusive nature of the gospel – not just the multiplicity of languages that were spoken at Pentecost, but, for example, in Acts 13.1 – 'Now in the church at Antioch there were prophets and teachers: Barnabas, Simeon who was called Niger, Lucius of Cyrene, Manaen a member of the court of Herod the ruler, and Saul' (Acts 13.1). Bruce Milne comments,

> The diversity of this Syrian congregation emerges in the description of the congregation's leadership team, five in number: Barnabas, from Cyprus; Simeon called Niger – 'the black', an African; Lucius of Cyrene – a North African; Manaen – possibly a slave of Herod's father, a Palestinian Jew; and Saul of Tarsus, a native of Asia Minor, the land bridge to Europe.[4]

The list is there for a reason – to show how the call of Christ is universal and how it is answered from every corner of the world. But in this as in so much else, Christianity has lost its original universality; it has to be rediscovered.

How are we to bring this about? The deeply damaging effects of imperial history are hard to overcome. And it is important not simply to throw out the cultural inheritance that we have – a church without history is like a person without memory. Each church is bound up with where it has come from, and although there are parts of its identity that are destructive and exclusive, there are other aspects that are to be treasured and celebrated.

There is a great deal of material available on this subject,

---

4 Bruce Milne, quoted in Linbert Spencer, *Building a Multi-ethnic Church*, 4.

and there is little point in repeating it here. Linbert Spencer has recently published *Building a Multi-Ethnic Church*, which includes detailed recommendations, but to move towards an inclusive church, four principal activities towards change can be identified in this as in almost any other area: welcoming, listening, learning and challenging.

First, welcome. It goes (almost) without saying that welcoming involves more than smiling at the door; it involves reaching out, making sure that people know that the church is open to them as well, responding when they come by visiting, asking, learning and repeating people's names, going to their celebrations and inviting them to yours. It involves having words of the liturgy in other languages, inviting people to wear their national dress, celebrating national days, sharing multinational food. It involves supporting people when they join committees for the first time, making sure that they are aware of meeting dates and times and offering, when possible, child care. It involves, in the end, letting people know that they are there not as honorary white British middle-class men but as Nigerians, Chinese people, Caribbeans, Germans, Americans, Medes, Parthians, from every nation, from all tribes and peoples and languages.

Second, listening. The mistake I made at St Peter's was to assume that because people were there, they were being heard. After many years, at a church council meeting, someone started speaking about 'Thanksgivings' – something of which I was not previously aware. In West African culture it is customary to give thanks in church for a happy event – the birth of a child, a marriage, a new job, a book contract. During the service the person giving thanks comes to the front, dancing and singing; and the family and friends come too. An offering of thanks is made, and the minister says a prayer. Simple; effective; necessary. But unknown to us despite many years of a Nigerian majority in our congregation. Similarly, the repeated requests for a Watch Night service on New Year's Eve had gone unheard. Everyone has something to contribute to the life of the church, but only if they are invited to, if the systems exist for them to be heard, and if the ways in which they are heard involve response.

Third, learning. Cultural and religious differences are very great, between the Caribbean and West Africa, between the United States and the UK, between the middle classes and the working classes. It was not until one of our leadership team went on a 'field trip' to West Africa that we realized how profoundly the West African understanding of spirituality differed from the English understanding – blessings and cursings are a routine part of everyday life in some parts of Nigeria, and the priest or minister has the job, or the power (sometimes at a price) of lifting curses. Some of our congregation come to St Peter's in the morning and go to a Pentecostal church in the afternoon, precisely because the Anglican Church does not offer the kind of spiritual interventions they believe are necessary for their own protection. This is not something we have yet been able to respond to fully; but at least we now know this is a concern. As we slowly develop a fuller understanding of the cultures of our congregations, we can enter more fully into the creative relationships with one another that the body of Christ needs in order to be healthy.

Fourth, challenging. 'We tried that, and they didn't come.' 'Nobody wants to stand for the PCC.' 'They're always late.' It may not work in all cases, but there was a tipping-point for us in the spring of 1999. The previous churchwardens were due to resign at the AGM, after 16 and 21 years' service respectively. New churchwardens were sought, and we were also looking for new parochial church council (PCC) members and others to be involved in the life of the church. Having asked around and not got much response, I decided to preach a sermon that not only encouraged but also challenged the black members of the congregation to come forward, saying 'This is your church too, and you all need to contribute ... There are two vacancies for churchwardens; it would be good if one of them was black.' Afterwards, I had a few negative comments; but I also had an immediate request to be churchwarden from Toro Erogbogbo, and she worked hard and excellently for the next six years. Our challenges in terms of timekeeping have been less successful; but that sermon was a key moment in creating a shared sense of ownership and responsibility across the congregation that has helped us to work together for the reign of God.

We still have a long way to go. We have no black or minority ethnic clergy, although the churchwardens and treasurer are from Sierra Leone and Ghana. Vocations over the last ten years have been exclusively white. In common with the rest of the diocese, British-born minority ethnic people are under-represented, and decisions still rest more with the white minority than with the whole congregation. But the changes over the past twenty years have been very great, and we are full of hope that as the life of the church goes on, and with God's help, the vision we have of full equality, of celebrating difference and of the creative life of the Spirit will begin to be fulfilled.

* * *

For many who have the straight rule of christendom applied in hurtful and destructive ways, the answer is to slam the book shut altogether and have nothing more to do with this story ... But for me that will not do ... I will not become a more flourishing person by cutting off my roots.[5]

The mutilation of the image of God, using only male language and metaphor to describe God in God's relationship with the creation, is the main reason for women's exclusion from ministry, simply because Christianity has been appropriated as a male religion. Women's ministry is such a deep issue that it goes beyond an eventual acceptance of women into priestly roles: it works as a challenge to structures of power, inside and outside the church.[6]

The task of including women in the life and work of our churches is very far from complete. Apart from the unfinished

5 Grace Jantzen, 'Contours of a Queer Theology', in Janet Soskice and Diana Lipton, *Feminism and Theology*, 345.

6 Marcella Althaus-Reid, *From Feminist Theology to Indecent Theology*, 27.

work of consecrating women as bishops within the Church of England and ordaining women as priests in the Roman Catholic Church, the subtle and not-so-subtle ways of ensuring that women remain disproportionately marginal to the churches' life are manifold. Liturgy and culture both send a message that, while women are welcome in the pews, their involvement too is conditional on good behaviour and not rocking the boat. God is exclusively masculine in the Church of England's liturgies as authorized in *Common Worship*; the structures and decision-making processes often work against the involvement of those with families, of principal carers, of people who work part-time because they have priorities elsewhere.

It would be wrong to say that this is intrinsic to Christianity, although the witness of scripture can scarcely be seen as anything other than overwhelmingly favouring the male over the female. But even someone as significant as Martin Luther occasionally acknowledges the potential equality of Adam and Eve, at least before the Fall: within his rigidly androcentric context, in his commentary on Genesis, he writes, 'Had the woman not been deceived by the serpent and sinned, she would have been in all things the equal of Adam ... [before sin] she was in no respect inferior to Adam, whether you count the qualities of the body or of the mind.'[7] Hardly a ringing endorsement of the equality of women, but indicative that neither scripture nor its interpretation in history is as monolithic as sometimes believed.

There is a huge amount of work on the writings of Paul with regard to women, and on how they may be interpreted, covering the spectrum of views from the most conservative to radically liberal. There is a disjunction between the radical inclusiveness of Paul, so clearly stated in Galatians 3.28 and reflected in the way in which Paul seems to engage as easily with women leaders as with men (Phoebe, Prisca, Aquila, Mary, Junia are referred to as equal to the men in Romans 16), and the instructions about the behaviour of women in church at, for example, 1 Corinthians 11.2–6 and 14.33–36. The apparent subordination

---

7 Janet Soskice and Diana Lipton, *Feminism and Theology*, 79.

of women to men is echoed by the writer of the Epistle to the Colossians, who reflects the radical equality of Galatians 3.28 but does not include women in his list – 'In that renewal there is no longer Greek and Jew, circumcised and uncircumcised, barbarian, Scythian, slave and free; but Christ is all and in all!' (Colossians 3.11).

It may be that this disjunction reflects two aspects of Paul's work and theology. His fundamental belief that in Christ *all* are a new creation is contrasted with his fervent concern for the preaching of Christ crucified and for the health of the communities for which he cares. 'Deep' Paul is at odds with 'public' Paul. His strictures on behaviour in liturgy and in church are the result of what he perceives to be dangerous anarchy – the grief he feels over divisions in the church and the great un-ease with which he views the behaviour of women are real, and they are part of his passion that Christianity should be a faith that all respect and to which all are called. As the feminist theologian Elisabeth Schüssler Fiorenza says, 'Paul is more concerned that order and propriety be preserved so that an outsider cannot accuse the Christians of religious madness.'[8] The world of the Spirit remains trammelled by the world of the flesh. Martin Luther echoes Paul when he says, 'If a woman wanted to be a man ... there would be a disturbance and confusion of all social stations, and of everything. In Christ, on the other hand, where there is no Law, there is no distinction among persons at all.'[9]

As an example of how the 'historical critical method' can negatively affect our understanding of scripture, this can hardly be bettered. For Paul, in the first century CE, the impression given to the outside world of female equality was potentially damaging to the preaching of the gospel. As a result, he includes strictures on behaviour that have been taken as normative ever since. How ironic it is that now, as a result of adherence to first-century expectations of the different roles of men and women, the church is perceived by the world as dangerously out of touch

8 In Janet Soskice and Diana Lipton, *Feminism and Theology*, 219.
9 Janet Soskice and Diana Lipton, *Feminism and Theology*, 86.

and misogynistic; so that the preaching of the gospel is undoubtedly undermined.

'For freedom Christ has set us free. Stand firm, therefore,
and do not submit again to a yoke of slavery' (Galatians 5.1).
In *From Feminist Theology to Indecent Theology*, Marcella
Althaus-Reid, an Argentine theologian presently Professor of
Contextual Theology at the University of Edinburgh, says,

> Reading Christ in the scriptures cannot be an exemplary but
> a revelatory reading. It is reading that unmasks that of God in
> Christ's own intimate chaos of love, messianic public expec-
> tations and contra/dictions that is the voice of subversion in
> an otherwise well-tamed text ... This is a Jesus who is greeted
> with kisses and a show of affection, but who is also betrayed,
> deserted and denied. The whole cycle of public humiliation,
> torture, laughter and derision ends with this poor, fragile
> young God dying a miserable death on the garbage dump of
> his city.[10]

It has been the function of western understanding of gender
differences over centuries to diminish the fullness of both men
and women by assigning specific roles to both. The route to
inclusion requires us to begin to conceive of the roles of women
and men in ways that go beyond assigned roles and into the new
world of love and freedom to which all are called by Christ.
As the centuries have progressed, the gender differences have
become more rather than less stark; with the rise of industrial
society and the advent of the nuclear family in the late eighteenth and early nineteenth centuries, the presence of women as
powerful prophetesses, abbesses or figures in history – Eleanor
of Aquitaine, Judith, Hildegard of Bingen – reduced. The patriarchal nature of the Christian community, which is a minority
voice in the New Testament (being found mainly in the later
Epistles) was emphasized after the Reformation, when the

---

10 Marcella Althaus-Reid, *From Feminist Theology to Indecent
Theology*, 168, 174.

'household' became the 'locus classicus' of Christian living.[11] Indeed the process of confining women to the household has proceeded to such an extent that, as Linda Woodhead suggests, 'The churches' stance on sexuality may have served to retain the loyalty of men and women wary of the subjective turn [within twentieth-century philosophy and theology] whilst alienating the larger numbers who find the prompting of the inner life more trustworthy than the imperatives of external obligation.'[12]

In the day-to-day life of the parish these considerations may seem far off, and yet they are deeply relevant. As much as anything else, the recognition of the effect of historic roles and expectations can enrich the life of the community. Again, the 'welcome, listen, learn and challenge' approach is helpful. Encouraging a diverse leadership team, ensuring that decisions are not taken in the pub of an evening instead of at PCC, enabling patterns of work and volunteering that respect school hours and shift patterns, making sure that the liturgy reflects diversity both in its language and in terms of who's involved and who's doing what – it all makes a difference. There is a nice irony in the fact that the Men's Group began shortly after the Mothers' Union, when we recognized that one part of the congregation that was receiving insufficient nurture was (mainly heterosexual) men. And although, at St Peter's, many of the jobs undertaken (flower arranging, maintenance) are mainly done by the groups one might expect, we hope that this is a result of a celebration of different skills and traditions rather than an assignation of strait-jacketing gender identities. We hope. What is vital, however, is that the gifts and talents people bring are increasingly recognized and welcomed as churches try to look beyond imposed categories of race or gender towards the person within, struggling to thrive.

* * *

---

11 Dale Martin, *Sex and the Single Savior*, 121.
12 In Gerard Loughlin, *Queer Theology*, 230.

But inclusion is not simply about race, gender and sexuality. A truly inclusive community tries to overcome the barriers created by age or youth, disability, class, wealth and poverty, education, and every other area where people are diminished or pushed to the margins by discrimination. Children and the elderly, people with visual impairment, and the biggest under-represented community in churches across the country – the white working class – what of them? And how do we ensure that the traditionally powerful do not experience a sense of exclusion as others find a place at the table?

An inclusive community is not a one-issue community, and each group within the church needs special recognition and special acknowledgement. An inclusive community also recognizes and celebrates different faith traditions, without collapsing inter-faith dialogue into an undefined mush; it acknowledges those who have no faith; and it tries to include those who are so convinced of the rightness of their own positions that they are unable to hear or respect the faiths of others.

It's a huge task, and no one can undertake it fully. Mistakes are good – we learn from them. And successes are good – we learn from them too. But in participating in the process, in trying to celebrate Life As She Is Lived, in welcoming, listening, learning and challenging, we are, each of us, in our own small ways bringing about the reign of God which is both among us and to come. Now we see in a mirror, dimly, but then we will see face to face. Now we know only in part; then we will know fully, as we have been fully known. And now faith, hope and love abide, and the greatest of these is love.

8

'Them out there, us in here'

Thomas Ernst is a consultant geriatrician at one of the London teaching hospitals. He and Tristan have been coming to St Peter's for five years. They held the celebration of their civil partnership there in 2006.

'We were led to St Peter's. I have no doubt. Tristan and I had always said we wanted to find somewhere to go to church. Then the flat came up in Walworth. I'd always been in a rush but this time I thought, no, let's wait and see if it's right. A week later it was still there, not expensive. I'd asked around and Peter told me that the church across the road was good – the Rector was gay and it was friendly and welcoming. So the first Sunday we'd lived there, we went. We walked in and I knew it was right. Sometimes we say, on a Sunday morning, "Let's not go to St Peter's, let's have a morning at home." But there's nothing to do, and we always end up going.

'I go there to worship. I very much enjoy serving and the spirit in the services, and God is definitely present there. But sometimes I think we don't say what it's about very well. It's all about love – we have to show the love – and sometimes I don't think people understand that. Some people didn't come to our civil partnership because it was in a church. That's so sad. Our friends are more Christian than some Christians I know, they just mistrust the church and authority for reasons we know only too well. It is the church's own fault. Our role is to change this, the tools we use are patience, persistence and love.

This is a lifetime mission for us. The church should ac-knowledge and preach that God's guidance and love is a free gift to everyone who believes in Love. This is why I think the church needs to do much more giving, much more. The people are the church. And the people are starving of love and revelling in material goods. Let us pray for them.'

Today the churches are undergoing fratricide over the issue of homosexuality, and the irony is that not just gays and lesbians, but the churches themselves, are likely to become the victims. The level of pure hatred, bitterness, closed-mindedness, and disrespect is staggering, going beyond any form of acrimony I witnessed over any issue since the struggle against racial segregation.[1]

The Anglican Communion is by no means the only church to be locked in controversy over lesbian and gay Christians. The Methodist and the United Reformed Churches have both had passionate and angry debates; the Roman Catholic Church has attempted to close down debate by dint of regular restatements from the Vatican of its position that homosexuality is an 'intrinsic moral disorder' and, by all accounts, a disproportionate amount of preaching time is taken up in evangelical and Pentecostal churches in condemning lesbian and gay people for their immoral lives. But it is writ most large within the Anglican Communion, and the controversy is being played out with painful slowness across the three continents of Africa, Europe and America, with the focus on the Bishop of New Hampshire, the Rt Revd Gene Robinson.

What is it about questions of same-gender relationships that has such power to destroy normal, courteous and generous discourse? Why is such hatred shown towards other Christians, particularly by conservative evangelicals, over this issue rather than any other? There have always been controversies in Christianity, from the very beginning; the Council of Jerusalem

---

1 Walter Wink, in *Homosexuality and Christian Faith*, vii.

between Paul and Peter and James was the first of many, many councils, formed at diverse times and in diverse places to define, redefine, anathematize or acknowledge new doctrines and new developments. Torture and burnings have been commonplace. But the urgent question facing the Anglican Communion at the moment, tragically in a world that faces increasingly desperate issues of poverty, disease and climate change, is whether a man in a relationship with another man may be a bishop, and whether two people of the same gender may have their relationship cele- brated in church. It is all the more surprising that this should be the case when the ordination of women – which has brought far greater changes to the church than any number of gay blessings – is being accepted with far less controversy and bile.

There is a toxic combination of factors that, shaken together and stirred, become explosive. Power and patriarchy, authority and freedom, identity, institutional integrity, scriptural inter- pretation and the place of the Bible, fear and welcome, love and disgust; all these and more are just below the surface of any discussion of lesbian and gay issues. Positions have over the past few decades become formalized and crystallized, to the extent that at times it seems as though no movement is possible and the church is doomed to be exclusive until the end of history.

For some, the question at issue is not so much about sexual- ity as about authority. The consecration of a gay bishop or the blessing of a same-sex relationship is seen as a radical departure from the witness of scripture, tradition and reason, and to make such a change is seen as undermining the authority of scripture and of the church. Rowan Williams said in the Archbishop of Canterbury's Advent Letter for 2007:

Our obedience to the call of Christ the Word Incarnate is drawn out first and foremost by our listening to the Bible and conforming our lives to what God both offers and re- quires of us through the words and narratives of the Bible. We recognize each other in one fellowship when we see one another 'standing under' the word of Scripture. Because of this recognition, we are able to consult and reflect together on the interpretation of Scripture and to learn in that process. Understanding the Bible is not a private process or something to be undertaken in isolation by one part of the family. Radical change in the way we read cannot be determined by one group or tradition alone.[2]

For others, the heart of the matter is about the sanctity of the sacrament of marriage; marriage is seen as the fullest expression of the relationship between Christ and his church, and exclusively between a man and a woman, so authorizing liturgies for gay or lesbian relationships would be profoundly transgressive and undermine the apparent witness of centuries.

But below and behind these questions of church order, authority and sacrament lies something more profound that continually re-ignites the debate over human sexuality in the church. A running theme of this book has been the constant dynamic tension between the individual and the community – the individual as created by God, and the community of Christ into which each individual is called. Questions of membership and welcome revolve around the way in which a person is perceived by a community and the community receives a person.

There is a danger, in the early twenty-first century, that we may take recent developments in society for granted. But the changes that have taken place over the last fifty years are little short of astonishing. In 1950 it would have been inconceivable that two of the most likely candidates in 2008 for the presidency of the United States would have been a woman and a black man. It would have been inconceivable that, however much work remains to be done, women and people from minority ethnic communities would have had full equality before the law in the United Kingdom, or even that people with disabilities would have the rights that are now enshrined in law. Power has, to an extraordinary extent, begun to move away from the traditionally powerful to groups that have until now had a place only on the margins of society.

Behind these changes, however, lie significant philosophical

2 Archbishop of Canterbury's Advent Letter, 2007.

developments. At risk of grossly oversimplifying, the intellectual history of the last six hundred years – since the Renaissance – has been one of gradually increasing differentiation and definition. The predominant concept of the Renaissance, expressed so clearly in Leonardo da Vinci's famous sketch of the 'ideal man' – the Vitruvian Man set simultaneously in a circle and a square – is that man (the male) is the measure of all things. The rise of modern scientific method and the increasing ability of human beings to measure, to experiment, to discover and to define led towards the Enlightenment, which liberated western thought from much of the mythological constraint under which it had laboured. With modern scientific method came the desire to define all things hierarchically; Linnaeus's categorizations of the natural world are an early example of attempts to classify the whole world, human and non-human. Each thing, each category was given its identity – the thousands of species of beetles and frogs were separately defined according to minute differences, and each had its own place in the hierarchy of being.

Modern gender studies have begun to identify the way in which the perception of women changed during and after the Enlightenment. Race, as a concept, emerges in the seventeenth and eighteenth centuries. Both gender and race become methods of ensuring that the hierarchy of power is maintained, with, at the top, the white, Anglo-Saxon, Christian, married father. The distinction between white and black, between male and female becomes sharper and sharper; the male is defined over against the female, the white man over against the black man, and the married man over against the single. The French philosopher Michel Foucault, in his classic study *Histoire de la Folie* (History of Madness), tracks the development of 'lunatic asylums', correlating their development precisely with the advent of the notions of sanity and madness as binary opposites; the sane are defined over and against the mad and the mad are locked away. According to Volf,

Much of Foucault's work consists in an attempt to explicate the exclusionary shadow that stubbornly trails modernity's history of inclusion – the institutions that we associate with civilisation shape 'normal' citizens with 'normal' knowledge, values and practices and thereby either assimilate or eject the 'ab-normal' other. The modern self ... is indirectly constituted through the exclusion of the other.[3]

The most recent categorization is equally insidious. The word 'homosexual' was coined in Germany in 1869 as a way of defining a sickness that had been identified: the sickness of sexual desire for a person of the same gender. Until then, there was no such categorization; there was, rather, the recognition that sometimes men had sex with men and sometimes women had sex with women. 'Sodomy' was considered a sin and often punished severely; but the creation of a category of person who was, by definition, different from the mainstream and also, by definition, sick, was new. Arnold Browne notes,

that the term ... was coined in 1869 is indicative of the development in the nineteenth century of the concept of two different sexual orientations ... If in the twenty-first century we are recognising that the spectrum of desires may be more complex, then we have been preceded by the ancient Greeks and Romans.[4]

The socio-political reasons for the creation of this new word and its rapid acceptance into mainstream discourse are not hard to find. Western society was, during the nineteenth century, probably more stratified and more patriarchal than at any time before or since. The rigidity of social categories, the rise of the nuclear family (as a result of the Industrial Revolution) and the global dominance of European empires gave the rich, white, western male more prestige than he had ever had. But conversely, as he became more powerful he also sought to fortify his power, and developed an intellectual and philosophical

---

3 Miroslav Volf, *Exclusion and Embrace*, 61, 62.
4 Arnold Browne, in Duncan Dormor and Jeremy Morris, *An Acceptable Sacrifice?*, 118.

structure to support his hegemony. The ubiquitous categorizations of 'race' in the nineteenth century were examples of this.
But whereas race and gender were easily visible and therefore
easy to identify, 'homosexuality' was, as a category, more hidden; it could be, so to speak, an enemy within the camp, seen
as dangerously undermining of the family and societal structures. The venom with which the Victorians sought to exclude
the homosexual is well known; we are living with the legacy of
that venom today.

Christianity has been pressed into action in support of in-
stitutionalized homophobia, as it has in support of racism and
sexism. The binary definition of male and female in Genesis 2,
for example, and the very few scriptural references to male–
male sex, have been ripped out of context and used to support
a worldview that has little to do with the Christianity of the
Gospels.

The traditional structures of power and influence are changing so radically at present that those who have enjoyed their
position at the top of the hierarchy are beginning to contem-
plate losing it. Or, at the very least, having to share it. At the
same time, the traditional certainties within society – the sup-
posedly complementary roles of men and women, the virtual-
ly unchallenged economic hegemony of western powers – are
also in flux. Many people welcome the changes that have taken
place since the Second World War; but for some, they are deeply
frightening.

The work of the French philosopher and intellectual René
Girard has been influential across academic disciplines. In Christian theology, James Allison's writings have brought Girard to a
wider audience in the English-speaking world, and there can be
little doubt that his notion of the 'sacrificial victim' in the context of Christianity has both enlarged and inspired a new and
deeper understanding of the place of Christ in contemporary
faith.

For Girard, the explicator of the way in which society functions is the mechanism of the sacrificial victim and its relationship to mimetic violence. His major works, including *Violence*

and the Sacred and *Things Hidden since the Foundation of the World* identify a process for the neutralization of the violence that seems to be endemic in society through shared participation in sacrifice. Very early societies, he says, were torn apart by the violence of 'mimetic desire' – it is part of the human condition to desire what one's rival has, whether it is a car, a woman or a piece of land, and the way to obtain this is usually through violence. Therefore disunity and dissension are written into the structures of all human societies. The way in which this disunity can be neutralized, in order that societies can avoid the descent into a perpetual spiral of violence and retribution, is by coming together to focus that violence on an external victim; a sacrificial victim. *Things Hidden since the Foundation of the World* develops an anthropology of religion identifying (a) that religion is intrinsic to society and (b) that sacrifice is intrinsic to religion, so it is through religious ritual in the form of sacrifice that warring parts of a population may come together in a show of unity.

> Polarised by the sacrificial killing, violence is appeased. It subsides. We may say that it is expelled from the community and becomes part of the divine substance ... for each successive sacrifice evokes in diminishing degree the immense calm produced by the act of generative unity.[5]

Girard has been an unfashionable sociologist; for many, this is because he sees the Christian story as being the key to the ending of the vicious circle of violence. Christ, as the perfect and cosmically innocent victim, shows the spiral to be the disaster that it is and brings it to an end. In other words, Christianity is at the heart of his philosophy, and the Eucharist (as the repeated celebration of the end of the sacrificial mechanism) is at the heart of Christianity.

There is, therefore, a savage irony in the fact that a very large

---

5 René Girard, *Things Hidden since the Foundation of the World*, 280.

part of the churches' present trouble over human sexuality is precisely because of the enactment of the victim mechanism. Those whose position in the hierarchy is most challenged at present – the traditionally powerful – have identified lesbian and gay people as an issue against which they can unite and seek to maintain their position. In the late twentieth and early twenty-first centuries, it is no longer acceptable to demonize or marginalize women or minority ethnic people in the way they were for so many centuries. But lesbian and gay people were until very recently a safe target – already on the margins of society and little understood, they could be attacked and undermined as a group, identified as 'perverts' or 'sick', as 'immoral', as 'intrinsically sinful' and therefore as a group to be excluded from the structures and ministry of mainstream churches. It is no accident that nearly all the most dominant players on the conservative side of the present arguments in the Anglican Communion – the funders, the masterminds and the activists – are white, male and married, either from the American Midwest or from England, and that the anti-gay movement is closely linked financially and in other ways to the neo-conservatives in the United States.[6] According to Dale Martin, 'contemporary Christianity in the United States ... has so closely aligned the basic message of Christianity with the family and "traditional family values" that it is currently in a state of idolatry'.[7]

There is a third reason for the current controversy. As well as the geopolitical changes that are taking place, and the superficially unifying working of the sacrificial mechanism, there are deep issues of purity and impurity at work. Just as, in former centuries, women menstruating were considered 'unclean' or marriages between people of different ethnic groups were illegal in many countries, so, now, lesbian and gay people have become the scapegoats in the desire for purity that seems so often to be linked with religious conviction. The laws in the Hebrew scriptures were created with the very specific aim of enabling the

6 For further information on this see 'Follow the Money' by Jim Naughton, available online via www.thinkinganglicans.net

7 Dale Martin, *Sex and the Single Savior*, 103.

people of Israel to keep themselves pure, and untouched by the ways of the peoples around them – the Canaanites, the Jebuzites, the Hittites, the worshippers of Baal. A great deal of the Holiness Code in Leviticus is to do with ensuring that the Israelites remain separate and identifiable: 'You shall keep all my statutes and all my ordinances, and observe them, so that the land to which I bring you to settle in may not vomit you out. You shall not follow the practices of the nation that I am driving out before you' (Leviticus 20.22–23). Despite the clear witness of the New Testament the need for definition against the outsider or against an Other remains; at present, for many on the conservative wing of the church, the 'other' is the 'homosexual'.

A fourth reason for the heat of this debate is the recent acceptance within parts of the church of the remarriage of divorced people. For very obvious reasons, many (not all) who take a conservative view on issues of human sexuality have found themselves moving on the question of the remarriage of divorced people, despite strong biblical injunctions against it. A sense of the need to hold on to the 'authority of scripture' has been undermined by this reinterpretation of what are generally accepted as the words of Jesus. The question of homosexuality is seen as a way in which, despite apparent movement on divorce and remarriage, a line can be drawn in the sand on the question of biblical authority.

Nowhere is the Bible more abused than in relation to human sexuality. A very few references to same-gender sexual relationships – Leviticus 18.22 and 20.13; Romans 1.27; 1 Corinthians 6.9–10; 1 Timothy 1.10 – are taken out of context by theologians and scholars who use them to justify a position that is, very profoundly, at odds with the message of Christ and of the scriptures. It is small wonder that the church is experiencing such difficulties over including lesbian and gay people when its foundation documents – the scriptures – are being so misused.

There is, however, general acceptance now that the Levitical references to same-gender sexual relationships are of limited usefulness for the conservative cause; there is too much in Leviticus that is now ignored (including, for example, the stoning of children for insolence) to enable a strong case for the observation of these two verses to be made. And the Greek words that are used in 1 Corinthians 6.10 (*arsenokoitai*) and 1 Timothy 1.10 (*malakoi*) are of too unclear a meaning to be applicable to twenty-first century situations – *arsenokoitai* appears to be closely related to Temple prostitution and *malakoi* to a form of effeminacy among men. Certainly neither mean 'lesbian' or 'gay' in the way in which these terms are understood in English.

Referring to Romans 1.27, Rowan Williams points out that the text is

> not helpful for a liberal or revisionist case, since the whole point of Paul's rhetorical gambit is that everyone in his imagined readership agrees in thinking the same sex relations of the culture around them to be as obviously immoral as idol-worship or disobedience to parents. It is not very helpful to the conservative either, though, because Paul insists on shifting the focus away from the objects of moral disapprobation in chapter 1 to the reading / hearing subject who has at this point been happily identifying with Paul's castigation of someone else ... Paul is making a primary point not about homosexuality but about the delusions of the supposedly law-abiding.[8]

It would be foolish to deny that where references are made to same-gender sexual relationships within the Bible, they are generally negative. But the mistake is to assume that this is as far as we can go on reading the Bible on these issues, and to treat these texts as 'proof texts' rather than listening to the witness of the scriptures as a whole. It is doubly ironic because, given that the writings of Paul are used more than any other references to exclude lesbian and gay people, the fact that Paul himself referred to the Hebrew scriptures in ways that are both creative and imaginative is completely ignored. Paul mines the

---

8 Rowan Williams, 'The Bible, Reading and Hearing', lecture given to Trinity College, Toronto, 16 April 2007.

Hebrew scriptures in a way common among the rabbinic community, using them freely to demonstrate and justify his belief that 'Christ is the end of the law' but what comes first is not the scriptures but Christ crucified and resurrected; what comes first is not the law but the saving event of Christ irrupting into the world.

A good example of this is the use by Paul of the Hagar and Sarah story in Galatians 3 and of the Ishmael and Isaac story in Galatians 4. Hagar, the slave girl of Abraham and her son Ishmael are in the original story the outsiders, cast out by Sarah and saved only by the grace of God; Sarah on the other hand gives birth to Isaac who is one of the patriarchs of the Hebrew scripture. Paul's wonderfully counterintuitive use of allegory and analogy, however, identifies Hagar and Ishmael with the Jews and Sarah and Isaac with the Gentiles.

Paul's passion for the gospel draws him on to use the scriptures freely and creatively, as a mine of allusion and story, of theology and godliness. He was steeped in the rabbinic tradition of interpretation of the Torah. The richness of the theology of the Epistles is closely bound up with the imagination with which Paul reads the Hebrew scriptures. As Richard Hays says: 'Only when our interpreters and preachers read with an imaginative freedom analogous to Paul's will Scripture's voice be heard in the church. We are children of the Word, not prisoners.'[9]

We are, therefore, able to move on from the rejection of lesbian and gay people implied by conservative interpretations of the scriptures, as we have moved on from racist and sexist interpretations of the scripture used to justify rejecting women and black people. We are freed to understand the witness and message of Jesus Christ as our primary authority, told to us through the Gospels and unfolded through the letters of Paul. The stories and miracles, the teaching and debates narrated in the gospel, the exegesis and passionate witness of Paul are our guiding lights as we seek to understand the faith we have been given. The inclusion of the outcast and the alien – the Samaritan

---

9 Richard Hays, *Echoes of Scripture*, 189.

woman, the woman with haemorrhages – the acknowledgement of Christ by Roman and Jew, slave and free, rich and poor; this is the overarching biblical narrative through which the present question of the inclusion of gay and lesbian people is to be understood.

According to Richard Burridge, the Gospels were written as biography to inspire us to imitate Jesus Christ; and the heart of Paul's theology, his letters and all his teaching is Christ, whom we are called to be like. 'An inclusive approach to New Testament ethics through the imitation of Jesus embraces all the canonical witnesses, that we might know the divine truth and love and share it with the whole of creation.'[10]

'Sexual difference is our modern obsession, the philosophical question that we must work out.'[11] There is, now, broad consensus among scientists, philosophers, policy-makers, legal establishments and society that orientation towards people of the same gender is and has always been an intrinsic part of any society, whether in the west, the east, modern times or prehistory. Reflected in the natural world, where same-gender sexual activity is if not frequent then at least regular, societies have found different ways to accommodate and at times welcome the sexual diversity in its midst. *Other Voices, Other Worlds*, edited by Bishop Terry Brown and subtitled 'The Global Church Speaks Out on Homosexuality', is a fascinating and at times inspiring collection of writings from places as far apart and as dissimilar as Uganda and Lakota members of the Sioux tribe in the USA. 'North' and 'south' are united in their recognition of the variety of sexuality and of relationships within not only Christianity but also Islam – 'As gay Muslims, we know too well the discrimination, homophobia and outright rejection that exists in our communities towards gay, lesbian, bisexual and transgendered (LGBT) people.'[12] The recent legislation on civil partnerships in the UK is part of a process in many countries across the world towards legal recognition of same-gender

---

10 Richard Burridge, *Imitating Jesus*, 346.
11 Jane Shaw, quoted in Gerard Loughlin, *Queer Theology*, 224.
12 Terry Brown, *Other Voices, Other Worlds*, 116.

relationships – for example full marriage, in Canada and Spain, or something similar to the UK's arrangement in Denmark and the Netherlands. But it is over the question of the affirmation of same-sex relationships that we hear the loudest calls from conservative theologians and Christians to be 'countercultural', to stand against the tide of modernism that, it is feared, may sweep away the foundations of society.

The cause of same-gender attraction is not yet fully understood. But it is increasingly clear that, just as some people beyond doubt experience gender dysphasia and are not complete until their gender is reassigned (transgendered people), and some people are born of indeterminate gender,[13] some are born with an intrinsic attraction to people of their own gender. And once it is accepted that this is the case, then there can be no acceptable Christian alternative to a generous welcome. The Christian vocation is to love, and loving means welcoming the created order.

A great deal of work has been published recently on the ethical and theological basis for acceptance – indeed for welcome – of LGBT people in the churches. Three collections of essays are particularly valuable – *Gays and the future of Anglicanism*, edited by Richard Kirker and Andrew Linzey; *An Acceptable Sacrifice?*, edited by Duncan Dormor and Jeremy Morris; and *Homosexuality and Christian Faith: Questions of Conscience for the Churches*, edited by Walter Wink. Beyond these relatively accessible books are more academic works such as *Sex and the Single Savior* by Dale Martin and *From Feminist Theology to Indecent Theology* by Marcella Althaus-Reid. Richard Burridge's book *Imitating Jesus: An Inclusive Approach to New Testament Ethics* provides an overview of current theological thinking in relation to the inclusive imperative within the New Testament, and while he applies this mainly to questions of

---

13 'The existence of inter-sexuality confounds the tidy categories that some Christian ethicists and church leaders work with and challenges us all to think more deeply about the God-given nature of our sexuality.' John Hare, in Duncan Dormor and Jeremy Morris, *An Acceptable Sacrifice?*, 99.

ethnic inclusion the parallel with LGBT people is specifically made.

There is a theological consensus of very considerable weight that, while differing in emphasis, is in broad agreement on three things: first, that same-gender attraction is rarely, if ever, a choice, and attempts to 'heal' same-gender attraction are, except in a few very limited cases, actively damaging; second, that the overwhelming theological and pastoral response should be not condemnation but a response of loving generosity; and third, that continuing rejection of lesbian and gay Christians is doing nothing but harm to the churches. An inclusive church is a welcoming church, and a welcoming church is a healthy church.

There are some who identify same-gender attraction with the Fall , and look to the eradication of homosexuality as one of the preconditions for the end-times, alongside the full reoccupation of Palestine by the Jews. But this circular argument depends on the perception of homosexuality as being intrinsically sinful; once it is acknowledged that it is simply a part of creation, it cannot then be identified with the Fall. There are others who resist 'the law of love' as a defining imperative for Christian behaviour – Richard Hays, for example, is concerned that love is 'easily debased in popular discourse ... a cover for all manner of vapid self-indulgence'.[14] But to assert that love is the same as 'vapid self-indulgence' is to misunderstand the extraordinarily demanding nature of the love to which Christians are called; the love that ends in the Cross and engages completely with the profound and challenging complexities of human nature.

Love is the beginning and end of the law, and a loving response to lesbian and gay Christians is not one that simply indulges; instead, it calls them as it calls all people to the higher and more difficult way of commitment and conviction to God and to one another. A loving response is bound to be complex. But love and condemnation are incompatible; telling people to reject their sexual orientation and deny their personhood before God is not and can never be the right way to live out the call of Christ.

---

14 Richard Hays, quoted in Richard Burridge, *Imitating Jesus*, 108.

The appeal to love will not solve all our problems or settle all our disagreements. But demanding that interpreters demonstrate that their condemnations of lesbian and gay Christians are 'the loving thing to do' is at least preferable to the simple statement that something is true just because 'the Bible says so' or because it is 'the will of God.'[15]

What would Jesus do? It's a good question; for if we are called to imitate Jesus we have to try to understand what Jesus is calling us to. And, given that, what should the churches do differently?

Tom Wright comments, 'There is a more or less universal consensus among scholars – something as rare as snow in mid-summer and no doubt similarly transitory – that Jesus offered a welcome to, and shared meals with "sinners".'[16] 'Sinners' in the context of the Gospels, are outsiders – those who are not part of the establishment or who by their behaviour have put themselves beyond the boundaries of cult or society. Prostitutes, tax collectors, outsiders. It is clear from the Gospels and from Paul's writings that Christ is calling his followers into the creation of a new community based not necessarily on blood connections but on a shared faith in the universal healing love of God.

Who is my mother, and who are my brothers?' And pointing to the disciples, he said 'Here are my mother, and my brothers! For whoever does the will of my Father in heaven is my brother and sister and mother.
Matthew 12.48–50

The radical nature of Jesus' call has been dulled over the centuries, but the letters of Paul bear witness to it – his fury at the Corinthians is due, among other things, to the fact that they are abusing the Lord's Supper by keeping the distinctions between rich and poor in the way they celebrate the Eucharist. 'What!

---

15 Dale Martin, *Sex and the Single Savior*, 168.
16 N. T. Wright, *Jesus and the Victory of God*, 294.

Do you not have homes to eat and drink in? Or do you show contempt for the church of God and humiliate those who have nothing? ... In this matter I do not commend you!' (1 Corinthians 11.22).

The first to acknowledge Jesus as the Christ in the Gospel of Mark is the Roman centurion – an outsider – and the one who encourages him to offer his ministry to the Gentiles is a Syro-Phoenician woman in Samaria. Jesus, in other words, was no respecter of external distinctions; all were equally welcome in the new community, the household of God. At the heart of his ministry and his work was the call to transformation – the 'contagious holiness' manifested in the healing of the woman with haemorrhages who is transformed by the touch of his garment.

In this context we can move on to my second question – what should the churches do differently? The answer is simple. We should treat LGBT people exactly as we treat everyone else. It is clear, if we are to live in imitation of Jesus, that we too should be no respecters of artificial boundaries, and that we should seek to offer the same sort of welcome that Jesus offered. Once we have accepted that some people are created to love people of their own gender, there is no possible justification for treating them any differently to anyone else in the world. The church is called to be alongside LGBT people as it is alongside married people, black people, rich people and poor people, encouraging them when they fall and challenging them when they fall away. Their relationships of love and growth are to be encouraged and their destructive acts are to be questioned. Their membership of the Christian community is to be affirmed, and their responsibilities as part of that community are to be made clear.

It will not, therefore, be a surprise if I say that we, as churches, should be celebrating the loving relationships of lesbian and gay people as we celebrate the loving relationships of opposite-gender couples. The church celebrates marriage because it reflects the love of God for God's church and the committed, constant and total love that Jesus Christ has for the people of God. The notion that supporting same-sex blessings in some way undermines heterosexual marriage is, as the former Bishop of Worcester points out, incoherent: 'I do not understand how my marriage can be undermined by two men down the road living in love together.'[17] On the contrary, affirming profound and committed relationships across society is likely to strengthen the status of marriage. The two services of thanksgiving for civil partnerships that we have held at St Peter's have been remarkable for the way in which the congregation, from government ministers to people close to the edge of society, were united in joy. It is, therefore, now urgent that the mainstream churches move towards authorizing a liturgy of thanksgiving for same-sex relationships or at the very least towards official recognition that these relationships have been celebrated by parish churches in different ways for very many years. The parallels with the service of thanksgiving after a civil marriage in the Church of England's *Common Worship* are very clear. Not everyone in the church is happy to remarry those who have been divorced, but a service has been authorized to be used by those who are. In precisely the same way, there should be a form of service that acknowledges a same-sex relationship and brings God into its heart.

Pending such a service being agreed (which may take some time) an inclusive church council should have a policy that enables a church to offer services to members of the congregation seeking to bring God into their relationship through prayer and thanksgiving. The canon that governs the Church of England's liturgy, Canon B5, authorizes the use of liturgy approved by the due processes of the church. But it also provides for a pastoral and liturgical response to particular situations where such a response is 'reverent and seemly and ... neither contrary to or in departure from the doctrine of the Church of England in any essential matter'.[18] Given that civil partnerships are specifically not marriages, given the Gospel imperative to celebrate the love of God wherever it is found, and given the pastoral responsibilities of clergy to their congregations and their parishes, it is

---

17 Peter Selby, *Gay Vicars*, Channel 4, 2007.
18 Canon B5 of the Church of England.

entirely appropriate for church councils to develop a policy that responds to the introduction of such partnerships.

It is equally urgent that the Church of England moves beyond the absurd situation it has got itself into over ordination and the consecration of bishops. The notion that lesbian and gay people can only minister to the church if they are in some sense forced publicly to embrace celibacy, whether this is their calling or not and regardless of how that affects both partners in a relationship, is deeply shocking in its pastoral insensitivity and a scar on the face of the church.

As in every other area, inclusion does not mean that 'anything goes'. Destructive, dishonest or careless behaviour is to be challenged in areas of relationships as much as anywhere else, and there is as much destructive behaviour among lesbian and gay people as there is elsewhere. But at least part of that is the result of the way in which society and the churches have forced gay and lesbian people to be secretive about who they are and therefore created an 'underground' sensibility. Work has not yet been done on how the civil partnership legislation is affecting LGBT people, but it would not be surprising if it brought about much change. Anecdotal evidence is that families and friends are supportive of civil partnerships in ways that previously were rare. The churches are almost alone among national institutions in their failure to respond.

Stumbling almost by chance into St Peter's on an ordinary Sunday, Jason Maldonado (whose story is at the beginning of Chapter 4) sat through most of the service perceiving and expecting rejection. That all changed when, in the Notices, the congregation was encouraged to pray for and support the Primates of the provinces of the Anglican Communion meeting at that time in Lambeth Palace, so that Anglican churches around the world could begin to offer a genuine welcome to lesbian and gay people. His expectations confounded, he became a member of the congregation and found his spiritual home.

The relative invisibility of LGBT people means that their simple presence in a church will not be enough to overcome the very real expectations of homophobia and rejection that are generally expected. Just as black people who have been historically excluded are loath to come forward for fear of further rejection, so too LGBT people will, with justification, stay away from church unless they are convinced that they will receive a genuine and profound welcome. Practical steps that can be helpful range from things as simple as having a clear mission statement or statement of faith on a church website and the noticeboard that is specific about the people welcomed: 'regardless of ethnicity, gender, marital status or sexual orientation'. It makes a difference when hundreds of years of prejudice is to be overcome. The acknowledgement of partners as partners and not as 'friends' matters too as a mark of respect for members of the church, with obvious implications, for example, for services celebrating civil partnerships.

Many LGBT Christians are people from an evangelical background who found, quite early on in their journeys into Christianity, that they were welcome only conditionally. Most gave up faith entirely – a few came through and found themselves back in the church but in a place that welcomes them. The spiritual and psychological damage, however, often runs deep. It is for this reason as much as any other that including LGBT people in a way that is both clear and reliable is essential. A hint of non-acceptance is enough to undo much good work – I remember once making a joke about how all the gay men were sitting together in church ('much better to keep them all in one place'), which came back to me only a fortnight later as an indication that the church was at heart homophobic.

In the end there are very few changes that are required of a local church beyond offering the sort of welcome that Jesus offered to those around him: unconditional, challenging, inspiring and trustworthy. The benefits are huge. People have gifts and talents, vocations and contributions. The more they are welcomed and brought into the heart of a church community the more they will offer and the more they will bring. Although many lesbian and gay people are deeply suspicious of the church, those who do find their way in often welcome it precisely because of the diversity present – the 'gay community' can be as oppressive as any other, and a change from that is both welcome and life-enhancing.

If, as quoted earlier, 'sexual difference is our modern obsession, the philosophical question that we must work out',[19] the acceptance of LGBT Christians is a large part of the working-out that needs to happen. But if that were to happen, the benefits for the gospel would be very great – not least because, at present, the place of sexuality in loving relationships is not something about which the churches can speak with much creativity or love. The many examples of permanent, stable and faithful relationships among clergy and lay people are unacknowledged and unaffirmed, and the ways in which God has moved in people's lives are unknown. It is a sad situation that stifles the work of the Spirit in churches and breaks down the relationship of trust between pastors and congregations. It is time for a change.

---

19 Jane Shaw, quoted in Gerard Loughlin, *Queer Theology*, 224.

9

My Space, Your Space

The drummers led the procession. They were from Creative Routes – a project run by and for people with mental health problems. Following them, as darkness fell, was a long line of lanterns, glowing in the dusk. A six-foot-long shark, light flickering out of its open mouth. A star. Another star. A batch of Chinese lanterns held high on bamboo poles. A moon, held high by a ten-year-old kid who had spent the last three weeks making it. Flowers, another fish, a space rocket. All constructed carefully by people of all ages, tissue paper stretched across willow and varnished, carried by mums and grans and kids and dads. African and English, Turkish and Canadian. Taxi drivers, unemployed people, classroom assistants, healthworkers.

We walked slowly from InSpire along the streets on to the Aylesbury, between Missenden and Latimer blocks, stopping in the new kids' play area to pick up more from the Aylesbury Youth Project, and back through the Octavia Hill Estate into the garden by the churchyard. By the time we reached the garden complete darkness had fallen. The procession climbed the mound in the centre. From the gates of the church I watched the massed lanterns lifted high in the night, surrounded by the lights of the Portland Street tower blocks and accompanied by the drums of Creative Routes.

This, I thought, was what we made InSpire for.

* * *

Inclusion is about more than people; it's also about how churches use their buildings. Every church that has a building is confronted with underlying questions about how its buildings can be used – are they a white elephant, draining resources and energy? Are they a cash cow, to be let to a nursery for commercial rent to cover the Diocesan Quota? Or are they to be used for other local people, which may produce less cash but meet more urgent needs?

A large part of the parish of St Peter's is made up of the Aylesbury Estate, a 1970s system-built local authority housing estate in the Borough of Southwark. In 1998, the residents of the Aylesbury Estate were in a mixture of despair and hope. Despair, because their bid to Europe for major funding had just been turned down. The bid was carefully put together and confidently submitted, after guidance from government. It offered a chance for the increasingly shabby and run-down estate to escape from its descending spiral, a noxious mix of fear of crime, abuse and physical neglect of the estate. It had the support of tenants, local authority and government. It failed.

Hope, because a new initiative had just been announced; and because the Prime Minister made the Aylesbury his first stop after the 1997 election. As a first step towards that, the Department of the Environment announced a pilot scheme called 'New Deal for Communities' (NDC), which would, it was hoped, offer some of the poorest and most deprived areas of the country a chance to turn themselves round. Local people were to be given the opportunity to bid for up to £57m to spend over ten years, on the priorities *they* identified, and to bring about the transformations *they* needed. What could be more full of hope?

Jean Bartlett, a grandmother on the estate, had the care of her young grandchild during the day. She realized that there were no care facilities available anywhere for the thousands of young mothers in the area. 'There was nothing for us,' she says. 'Everything we did we had to fight for. When I set up Little Tykes, no one would listen at first.' The Aylesbury Estate had quickly stopped being a place of hope and become a place 'notorious' for its crime and drug problems, for the teenage pregnancy statistics, for high unemployment and poor health; a nexus of problems apparently intractable.

The congregation of St Peter's were wondering what the future held for them. The Sunday congregation had been running on empty for some time, despite the hard work of a few key members, and was unsure about its future. The damp and the cold as winter set in filled me, as the new parish priest, with anxiety. The building seemed too big for the congregation; the churchyard was a wilderness.

I'd been given the specific responsibility, as part of my appointment, of working with the people of the Aylesbury Estate to support them in the plans for their homes and their communities. But what did this mean? What were we going to do with the building? How were we to speak of love in Walworth?

With the help of and funding from Business in the Community, we carried out an independent audit of local needs. We interviewed residents and members of the church. We sent out 500 surveys and had a good return. We talked to community groups and local service providers, and we reviewed the statistics.

We discovered that Faraday Ward was among the 10 per cent most deprived in the country, that 33 per cent of residents were on income support and 23 per cent lone parents, that 7 out of 10 unemployed people had not worked in over two years and that other key education and health indicators were among the poorest in the country. Key areas where the need for help and support was identified were: basic skills, English as a second language and IT training, careers advice/job seeking and parenting support.

None of this was surprising; it confirmed the preconceptions we had about the parish. But further investigation of the situation showed us that the superficial statistics tell only a tiny part of the story. The impression began to form of something profoundly solid and deeply impressive, below the waterline and invisible. We had an idea of that from the residents of the Aylesbury who came to church – many of whom had lived on the estate for over 30 years. But the reconnaissance we carried out gave weight and breadth to our impressions, and changed the way we understood our responsibility as a parish church.

A 'Mutual Aid Survey' was carried out in early 1999. The Borough of Southwark commissioned the project, to identify the extent of mutual aid – help and support between neighbours – that took place on the Aylesbury Estate. It uncovered some statistics that surprised us: 90 per cent of people gave help or support to a neighbour; 81 per cent received help or support from a neighbour; 47 per cent had lived on the estate for more than ten years; 20 per cent gave or received help from a relative also living on the estate; three-quarters were in some sort of regular, routine, informal helping relationship; 18 per cent attended a place of worship locally; 18 per cent were involved in their tenants' association; and 63 per cent wanted to return there after any redevelopment.

In other words, the Aylesbury did not conform to the stereotype of a run-down, inner city estate. While for some people the sense of isolation was strong, there also existed a diverse, confident and supportive community, unsung and unacknowledged. A community that had not had the chance to raise its head above the parapet; it had been characterized by struggle rather than success, by crime instead of creativity. Overwhelmingly, when people were asked what they thought the area needed, they responded with something along the lines of – a place to meet, a place for learning, somewhere for arts and creativity.

We realized that one of the problems for Aylesbury residents was that the community as a whole had few meeting places – those that existed were small and shabby tenants' halls with limited access – and that people living on, and around, the estate had few opportunities to meet together to develop the sorts of activities that contribute greatly to quality of life and depth of community.

We had a semi-derelict, listed building designed by Sir John Soane. It represented both a privilege and a responsibility. Having begun to identify needs we commissioned feasibility studies, asking our architects to provide a space big enough for 150 people to meet together with smaller spaces for different activities. It was fundamental to our brief that the worship space – remarkable in its beauty and offering a space for performance and prayer – should remain unaltered. But apart from the worship space there was nowhere large enough for more than ten people to meet comfortably.

The plans, as they emerged, were dramatic. Clearing the whole crypt back to its fundamental structure, removing the post-war accretions, opening up the lightwells to bring in natural light, creating north–south and east–west vistas, exposing the original brickwork and opening up spaces for people to meet, dance, talk, create, learn and flourish. The plans offered a transformation of a space originally intended (literally) for death into a space for life. They built on the crypt's history – in 1895 the Revd Canon William Horsley cleared it of the 'two hundred and fifty bodies strewn about the crypt in a most insanitary fashion according to the customs of our forebears' and began to use it for school meals. Since then it had acted as a soup kitchen, an air raid shelter (and took a direct hit, with many deaths resulting), and as a social club.

At the heart of the project was the awareness that the whole area was to be completely transformed over the next ten years. The NDC proposals were for a total demolition and rebuild of the Aylesbury. London south of the Thames is undergoing fundamental changes – the City is reaching further and further south, and the Elephant and Castle, only 500 yards from St Peter's parish boundary, was also to be completely redeveloped over the next ten years.

At heart, we saw the need to provide a place of continuity in the midst of massive change. A place of celebration, of excellence and of light. Somewhere that people could rely on, but also somewhere that felt good, felt like a place of welcome, felt like somewhere that hadn't been cobbled together on the cheap and funded badly. Somewhere people left feeling better than they had when they arrived – a place where outsiders could be included and where different members of different communities could encounter each other in a way that was neither threatening nor suspicious.

Gradually, through research, analysis, conversation, dreaming and praying, the vision for the place emerged. The working

group charged with the project came up with a mission statement: 'Our mission is to build up this community, seek justice
for people on the edge and serve those in need in Walworth and
beyond.' From the mission statement came the name: InSpire,
and the aim: 'InSpire aims to be a centre for learning where local
people can creatively and imaginatively obtain new skills, increase their self-confidence and develop a sense of community.'

The next two years were the busiest part of the project, for the
people of St Peter's. But after a great deal of negotiation, hus-
tling, fundraising, heartache and drama, InSpire was dedicated
by the Archbishop of Canterbury on 31 October 2003. With the
paint still wet (literally), the Centre swung into action.

The speed with which InSpire became a key part of the local
community was remarkable. With the support of Southwark
Council, who immediately began to use it for meetings and con-
ferences; with a café that (although not quite up to the standard we were hoping for) was offering good food at reasonable
prices; with good IT and close co-operation with partners including Sure Start, the NDC and the Prince's Trust; our dream
of inclusion and imagination began to become real. We aimed
to be both rooted and creative. One of the most constructive
initiatives has been the close partnership with the Prince's Trust,
who offer a twelve-week course around confidence-building,
teamwork and practical skills to 'NEETS' – young people who
are not in employment, education or training. The English as a
Second Language and Information Technology courses are well
subscribed. But these are run closely alongside the more obvi-
ously creative work – music, art and drama – so that the same
people are involved in activities beyond their original intentions.
Jade, for instance, started on the Prince's Trust course and is
now training in childcare, having helped out at the children's
Summer School. In November 2005 2InSpire was opened. It's
on the Aylesbury Estate, in a specially equipped performance
space that had not realized its potential since its creation at
considerable cost ten years before. 2InSpire hosts the Aylesbury
Choir and line dancing. It also does detailed and intensive work
around music and dance with young people on the estate, and

is about to start an NVQ in hairdressing in response to the requests of those same young people.

I take from conversations with Ann Morisy the idea of churches offering a place of 'alternative performance'. A place beyond the imperative of 'profit, power and status'. Without being intended, it seems that that has happened at InSpire. Although it's not directly associated with the church – many see it as simply sharing premises – our underlying intention, to offer a place where people can 'creatively and imaginatively obtain new skills, increase their self-confidence and develop a sense of community', has led to precisely that sense of alternative performance; of people meeting in different ways on different levels, across the boundaries of class, age, gender, sexual orientation and ethnicity. We have good links with the Southwark-funded lesbian and gay group, who make their carnival floats in InSpire; and with the over-60s bingo group.

Sitting at the heart of InSpire it's easy to get things out of proportion. But it does, tentatively, appear that it has begun to offer the place of continuity we hoped to offer as redevelopment begins. Beyond doubt, people involved at InSpire see it as a place they can be proud of, which offers hope and constancy in a time of change.

How has InSpire affected the church itself? The church's own mission statement begins 'We aim to be open, caring and prayerful.' It's difficult to say what the direct connections have been. But the congregation is larger and more confident that it was when we started. The church building is back at the heart of the community. The receptionist of InSpire now comes to church every Sunday, and the parish administrator works very closely with InSpire. Members of the church work in InSpire and attend its courses, and people from InSpire come into church to work, to play and to pray.

The partnership has been a dramatic outworking of the church's sense of its own mission. Put at its simplest, our intention was to include the local community we serve. Through providing InSpire, the building and resources are placed at the service of local people. It is one way in which the church can try to live out the inclusive gospel in South London. Who knows what, in 100 years' time, will have taken the place of InSpire – or whether St Peter's will still be a church. In the meantime, however, the church takes heart from the out-working of the vision of alternative performance.

A mosaic course is run at InSpire by a local artist who lives on the Octavia Hill Estate. Topps Tiles held a mosaic competition, and the pieces made were entered. One piece was made by an Aylesbury resident who is also a refugee. The judge's comments on his entry perhaps sum up the meaning of InSpire –

The indoor wall piece is one of very few portraits ever submitted for the award and what a splendid piece of work it is. Unfussy but wonderfully expressive, set just off centre using a perfectly balanced colour scheme. I think it is the head of Jesus but apologise if I am wrong. Very well done indeed, this impressive portrait wins the award.

Conclusion: The Future is Bright

I am black and beautiful, O daughters of Jerusalem, like the tents of Kedar, like the curtains of Solomon. Do not gaze at me because I am dark, because the sun has gazed on me. My mother's sons were angry with me; they made me keeper of the vineyards, but my own vineyard I have not kept! Tell me, you whom my soul loves, where you pasture your flock, where you make it lie down at noon; for why should I be like one who is veiled beside the flocks of your companions?
Song of Solomon 1.5–7

The breathtaking poetry of the Song of Solomon bears constant rereading. At the heart of the scriptures is a song of sensuality and love:

My beloved speaks and says to me: 'Arise, my love, my fair one, and come away; for now the winter is past, the rain is over and gone. The flowers appear on the earth; the time of singing has come, and the voice of the turtledove is heard in our land.'
Song of Solomon 2.10–12

It's like a depth charge planted in the heart of the Old Testament, waiting to be uncovered so that the untrammelled passion of the words can be allowed to sing again. Yet it rarely appears in our lectionaries and we rarely hear its music.

There is a well-known poem by Gerard Manley Hopkins:

Glory be to God for dappled things –
For skies of couple-colour as a brinded cow;

{135}

For rose-moles all in stipple upon trout that swim;
Fresh-firecoal chestnut-falls; finches' wings;
Landscape plotted and pieced –
fold, fallow, and plough;

And áll trádes, their gear and tackle and trim.
All things counter, original, spare, strange;
Whatever is fickle, freckled (who knows how?)
With swift, slow; sweet, sour; adazzle, dim;
He fathers-forth whose beauty is past change:
Praise him.[1]

The politics and the debates, the anxiety and the arguments smear the vision of the new creation. Where we find all things counter, original, spare, strange; where we find the lovers of the Song of Solomon and the squabbling people of Corinth, the stern reformers of the sixteenth century and the ecstatic mystics of Catholic Spain, the hard-working inner-city Oxford Movement priests of the 1860s and the passionate evangelicals of the beginning of the twenty-first century. Not to mention the millions of people seeking God in other ways or not seeking God at all, but living for the reality of love experienced in a million different ways.

Christianity as a faith contains both transcendence and immanence. Running through its core is the notion of God both as completely other ('He fathers-forth whose beauty is without change') and God as utterly present – a squalling baby in the manger in Nazareth. The impassable and the abundantly human. But our earthbound lives, the work and ministry of our churches, leave us at the end of every day exhausted, worn out with meetings and negotiations, disputes lost and won, solutions tried and failed or tried again. For the want of a vision the people perish.

For this reason, if for no other, there is little more important than the moments of encounter, the fleeting glimpses of a bet-

---

1 Gerard Manley Hopkins, 'Pied Beauty'.

ter world when the curtain is drawn back and we begin to see what Jesus might have meant. Inclusion is part of that vision; for inclusion celebrates difference without belittling anyone, and allows each person to come to the altar as they are, transformed and yet the same, both Christ-like and human. 'A new heart I will give you, and a new Spirit I will put within you: and I will remove from your body the heart of stone and give you a heart of flesh' (Ezekiel 36.26).

We are entrusted with a diamond, but we are fearful of letting it be seen. The radical gospel message of God's unconditional love is rarely heard. Now, perhaps, more than ever, we have a gift to offer those around us. We are being challenged to allow the voice of love to be heard in a world where weeds are growing up and choking the corn, ravens eating the seed and the roots are withering. At the moment, the voice of love is whispering, in secret, away from the highways and byways. Are we willing to allow it to sing?

Bibliography

General

Fraser, Giles, *Christianity with Attitude*, Norwich, Canterbury Press, 2007.

Ignatieff, Michael, *Magnum*, London, Phaidon, 2000.

Kline, Nancy, *Time to Think: Listening to Ignite the Human Mind*, London, Cassell, 1999.

Patey, Edward, *Faith in a Risk-Taking God*, London, DLT, 1991.

Pritchard, John, *The Life and Work of a Priest*, London, SPCK, 2007.

Sachs, Albie, *The Soft Vengeance of a Freedom Fighter*, Berkeley, University of California Press, 2000.

Simmons, Michael (ed.), *Street Credo*, London, Lemos & Crane, 2000.

Torry, Malcolm, *Regeneration and Renewal*, London, Canterbury Press, 2007.

Young, Michael and Peter Willmott, *Family and Kinship in East London*, London, Penguin Classics, 2007.

Theology and Philosophy

Alison, James, *Undergoing God*, London, DLT, 2006.

Alison, James, *Faith Beyond Resentment*, London, DLT, 2001.

Baudrillard, Jean, 'The Evil Demon of Images', in Thomas Docherty (ed.), *Postmodernism: A Reader*, New York, Columbia University Press, 1993, 194–200.

Burridge, Richard, *Imitating Jesus*, Cambridge, Eerdmans, 2007.

Fraser, Giles, *Redeeming Nietzsche*, London, Routledge, 2002.

Girard, René, *Things Hidden since the Foundation of the World*, London, Continuum, 2003.

Girard, René, *Violence and the Sacred*, London, Continuum, 2005.

Gutiérrez, Gustavo, *The God of Life*, London, SCM Press, 1991.

Gutiérrez, Gustavo, *A Theology of Liberation*, London, SCM Press, 2001.

Hays, Richard, *Echoes of Scripture in the Letters of Paul*, New Haven, Yale University Press, 1989.

John, Jeffrey, *The Meaning of the Miracles*, Norwich, Canterbury Press, 2001.

Kirwan, Michael, *Discovering Girard*, London, DLT, 2006.

Kristeva, Julia, *Strangers to Ourselves*, New York, Columbia University Press, 1991.

McFague, Sally, *Metaphorical Theology*, Philadelphia, Fortress, 1982.

Moltmann, Jürgen, *The Crucified God*, London, SCM Press, 1974.

Morisy, Ann, *Journeying Out*, London, Continuum, 2004.

Myers, Ched, 'A House for All Peoples? A Biblical Study on Welcoming the Outsider', *Sojourner*, April 2006.

Newman, John Henry, *An Essay on the Development of Christian Doctrine*, London, James Toovey, 1845.

Nietzsche, Friedrich, *The Antichrist*, London, Penguin, 1990.

Nouwen, Henri, *In the Name of Jesus*, London, DLT, 1989.

Peck, James, *The Chomsky Reader*, London, Serpent's Tail, 1988.

Rorty, Richard, *Philosophy and Social Hope*, London, Penguin, 1999.

Rorty, Richard, *Contingency, Irony and Solidarity*, Cambridge, Cambridge University Press, 1989.

Shakespeare, Steven and Hugh Rayment-Pickard, *Inclusive God*, Norwich, Canterbury Press, 2006.

Volf, Miroslav, *Exclusion and Embrace*, Abingdon, Nashville, 1996.

Walls, Andrew, *The Cross-Cultural Process in Christian History*, Edinburgh, T&T Clark, 1992.

Ward, Keith, *Rethinking Christianity*, Oxford, Oneworld, 2007.

Wink, Walter, *Engaging the Powers*, New York, Galilee Press, 1999.

Wright, N. T., *The Climax of the Covenant*, London, Augsburg Fortress, 1992.

Wright, N. T., *Jesus and the Victory of God*, London, SPCK, 1996.

Ethnicity, Sexuality, Gender

Althaus-Reid, Marcella, *From Feminist Theology to Indecent Theology*, London, SCM Press, 2004.

Brown, Terry (ed.), *Other Voices, Other Worlds*, London, DLT, 2006.

Dormor, Duncan and Jeremy Morris (eds), *An Acceptable Sacrifice?*, London, SPCK, 2006.

Good, Deirdre, *Jesus' Family Values*, New York, Seabury, 2006.

Griffin, Horace, *Their Own Receive Them Not*, Cleveland, Pilgrim, 2006.

Holloway, Richard, *Anger, Sex, Doubt and Death*, London, SPCK, 1992.

BIBLIOGRAPHY

Linzey, Andrew and Richard Kirker (eds), *Gays and the Future of Anglicanism*, Winchester, O Books, 2005.

Loughlin, Gerard (ed.), *Queer Theology*, Oxford, Blackwell, 2007.

Maitland, Sara, *A Map of the New Country*, London, Routledge & Kegan Paul, 1983.

Martin, Dale B., *Sex and the Single Savior: Gender and Sexuality in Biblical Interpretation*, Louisville, Westminster John Knox Press, 2006.

Robinson, Gene, *In the Eye of the Storm*, Norwich, Canterbury Press, 2008.

Soskice, Janet and Diana Lipton (ed.), *Feminism and Theology*, Oxford, Oxford University Press, 2003.

Spencer, Linbert, *Building a Multi-Ethnic Church*, London, SPCK, 2007.

Wink, Walter (ed.), *Homosexuality and Christian Faith: Questions of Conscience for the Churches*, Minneapolis, Fortress, 1999.